INTERNATIONAL EDUCATION:
The Unfinished Agenda

Edited by
William C. Olson, Dean
School of International Service
and
Llewellyn D. Howell
Professor of International Relations
The American University

With a Foreword by
Rand V. Araskog
Chairman and President
ITT Corporation

White River Press, Inc.
Indianapolis, Indiana

Copyright © 1984 by White River Press, Inc.
Printed in the United States of America
All rights reserved. No part of this book shall be reproduced or transmitted in any form or by any means, electronic or mechanical, including photocopying, recording, or by an information retrieval system, without written permission from the Publisher:

White River Press, Inc.
1857 North Pennsylvania Street
Indianapolis, Indiana 46202

First Printing 1984

Library of Congress Cataloging in Publication Data

Main entry under title:

International Education: The Unfinished Agenda

(The ITT key issues lecture series)
1. International education—United States—Addresses, essays, lectures. I. Olson, William C. II. Howell, Llewellyn D. III. Series.
LC1090.1556   1984   375′.0082   84-52254
ISBN: 0-932431-00-3

Contents

Preface

Richard Berendzen
President
The American University

International education should be at the very heart of the curriculum—for students in business, government service, economics, history, art, philosophy, even science. Whether your ultimate field will be communications or law, an international perspective is essential.

Part of the problem with international education in the United States is that, while we know it should be comprehensive, we often have defined it too narrowly. If you look up "university" in the *Oxford English Dictionary*, you will find that it shares origins with "universe." It means universal, to embrace all there is. That is the challenge of educators: to instill in students a sense of living, working, and contributing in the total world rather than just at home.

I have had the honor of traveling to a number of countries, and sometimes my experiences have been enriching, sometimes eye-opening.

A few years ago, Kuwait—the tiny, wealthy, progressive nation—asked me to speak in a lecture series. Realizing that I was scheduled on the eve of Albert Einstein's birthday, I asked the Kuwaitis, "Would you mind if I included in my address a tribute to him?"

I was anxious about their response, because Kuwait has one of the highest numbers of Palestinians per capita in the world, nestled as it is next to Saudi Arabia, Iraq, and Iran. The person I wished to honor had been offered the first presidency of Israel.

Well, their instant response was, "Wonderful. Einstein was a great scientist and an inspiring philosopher. We admire him deeply, so why don't you do that?"

I stood in the vast hall, looking out on a thousand people wearing throbes and bishts as I attempted to explain about the universe and the contribution of this remarkable man. Afterwards, dozens of appreciative members of the audience came up to ask questions, and it took two hours to get out of the hall.

Once again, I was convinced that, while there is distrust, hatred, and war, some things transcend such horrors. One of them is mutual, universal respect for the exceptional contributions by good people. And a key way to learn about that is through international exchange and education.

To both Dean William C. Olson and Professor Llewellyn D. Howell goes our deep appreciation, for this series has enabled The American University to enhance its role in advancing public understanding of major contemporary issues.

I add also an expression of appreciation to the executives of the ITT Corporation for their interest in the School of International Service and its educational mission.

Foreword

Chairman, President and Chief Executive
ITT Corporation

As our world becomes a more interconnected and interdependent place, the need for a better understanding of other cultures has never been greater. In fact, international involvement is basic to the very idea of a university.

Yet it has been foreigners—approximately 340,000 of whom are studying in the United States—who readily have seized the opportunity. Since 1949, more than two million students from developing countries have studied here. It is estimated that almost half the scholars throughout the world who are studying outside their own country gravitate to the more than 2,500 colleges and universities in the United States.

But it has been a two-way process. Since the early part of the century, some of our most capable public servants were among the 32 Americans receiving Rhodes Scholarships annually. In Chapter 1, Richard T. Arndt estimates that by 1911 there were 5,000 American students in Europe, and 10,000 in 1930, and probably well over 400,000 Americans are studying abroad today. And the Fulbright Fellowships, created in 1946, have enabled more than 50,000 Americans to study and teach abroad. The Fulbright program has expanded to 120 countries and is a proven instrument of our public policy.

What kind of internationalized world will the coming generation inherit? I share Sven Groennings' optimism in Chapter 4 that America's universities will have more worldwide influence in the decade ahead.

As the chief executive of the largest international manufacturer of telecommunications equipment, I can assure you that advances in digital technology, satellites, and computers are revolutionizing the way we accumulate, store, and transmit information. We now have the means to encompass every university and research center in a global web of shared knowledge. That capability also increases the potential for intercultural understanding.

In my travels to ITT manufacturing and service operations in some 100 countries, I've noticed another positive factor about the new technology in telecommunications that is often overlooked. It is creating thousands of interesting jobs that are more challenging and ego-satisfying than the majority of jobs in those countries.

Dean Olson and Professor Howell, who moderated the series, are to be commended for bringing together an excellent group of nationally-known thought leaders. This volume should help clarify the policy issues facing a world that has moved a long way toward interdependence, and it should serve as a timely contribution to the literature of international education.

The School of International Service at The American University was a fitting campus locale for the tenth anniversary celebration of the ITT International Fellowship Program administered by the Institute of International Education. We at ITT are indeed proud that this program has enabled almost 600 students from the United States and other countries to study abroad.

Introduction

William C. Olson and Llewellyn D. Howell

Dr. William C. Olson is dean of the School of International Service at The American University in Washington, D.C. Dr. Olson served in military intelligence in the European theatre during World War II. He later taught political science at Yale while completing his Ph.D. in international relations and subsequently taught at Pomona and the Claremont Graduate School. Dr. Olson became Chief of the Foreign Affairs Division, Legislative Reference Service, Library of Congress, in 1961, where he served until 1965, when he became associate dean of the Faculty of International Affairs and senior lecturer in government at Columbia University. In 1967 he was appointed associate director for the social sciences of the Rockefeller Foundation and in 1970 became director of the foundation's Bellagio Study and Conference Center in Italy. He became Dean of The American University's School of International Service in 1979. He has been the president of the International Studies Association, and a member of the board of trustees of the Experiment in International Living, and is currently a member of the board of trustees of the Graduate School of International Studies in Denver. Dr. Olson is coauthor and coeditor of The Theory and Practice of International Relations, *now in its sixth edition, and the author of numerous articles on American foreign policy and international relations.*

Dr. Llewellyn D. Howell is professor of international relations at the School of International Service, The American University, and is the Washington, D.C., area coordinator for the Foreign Policy Association's Great Decisions Program. He was a Peace Corps Volunteer in Malaysia from 1963 to 1965 and has served in the Department of State and the Department of Defense. After receiving his Ph.D. in International Relations from the Maxwell School at Syracuse University, he taught at the University of Hawaii at Hilo and Manoa before coming to The American University in 1974. Dr. Howell has conducted field research in the ASEAN states of Southeast Asia, in Central America, and in West Africa, as well as opinion and attitude research in the United States. He is the author of more than thirty journal articles on international relations and is currently at work on a text, Understanding International Relations: Actors, Issues, Events. *He specializes in public opinion on American foreign policy.*

WHAT IS INTERNATIONAL EDUCATION?

One reason this volume carries the subtitle *"An Unfinished Agenda"* lies in the fragmented nature of the field. Everyone seems interested in educating someone else about things international, but few seem aware of what others are doing or trying to do. It is inevitable that some are duplicating the work of others and that some are at cross-purposes with one another, all of which results in many well-intentioned individuals and groups achieving less than their efforts deserve.

What is needed, we concluded, is a new attempt to define the purposes of international education, which in turn reveals how many different ways the subject can be approached. Among those which readily come to mind are the growing international concerns of teachers and other professional educators at all academic levels, including the increasing attention being given to comparative education.

Almost equally obvious are the widespread efforts being made, both by private groups with a special axe to grind on behalf of some countries and by those who are concerned about the quality and direction of our foreign policy, to educate the citizenry about international affairs, but with a particular point of view in mind for promotion. The obverse side of this coin can be seen in the prodigious activity of those public officials who make foreign and defense policy and explain it to the public. Policy and/or political support is the goal under this definition.

Yet another approach manifests itself in the graduate programs of the professional schools of international affairs whose purpose is to train not only diplomats but also thousands of others whose careers will take them overseas. Undergraduates as well are exposed to a panoply of courses in world politics, although extent and quality vary widely. Foreign language training is being encouraged after a long period of cutbacks by hard-pressed school boards determined to eliminate "frills"— frills upon which, in the case of Americans about to communicate abroad, our very security may depend.

Thousands of students cross the ocean annually to study in countries other than their own. Some do so only for cultural exposure; others choose this as the route to professional competence in their chosen fields. Fulbright and ITT Scholarships promote these exchanges on a systematic basis, as do study-abroad programs and "London Semesters" such as those we have at The American University.

Foreign tourism, whatever the legitimate commerical purposes of travel agents may be, is an educational experience, whether the tourist realizes it or not. Similarly, business executives and members of the military who are stationed abroad learn much about the world through their encounters. That this education is mostly accidental rather than organized remains the issue particularly when so many who serve abroad have been taught practically nothing about it.

By contrast, in their organized approach to education, scientists have long regarded science as being by its very nature international. The mutual education which takes place constantly through worldwide professional associations has in some ways the most far-reaching effects on the future of mankind of any of the manifold forms of international education.

The large immigrant population in the United States, and the many issues that swirl around it provide a firsthand international education without ever leaving home. This is again, however, a case of international education by coincidental encounter rather than by systematic programs, which does little to alleviate the problems of understanding that we face and may indeed even exacerbate them. Contact sometimes breeds mistrust rather than friendship.

We cannot forget that international education is not simply a one-way process and that other nationalities must also learn about Americans and the United States, as well as about each other. Thus, both Americans traveling and studying abroad and those of other nationalities undertaking similar activities in the United States further the cause of a *mutual* international education.

The list could be extended, but the agenda is indeed unfinished, as this series of *Key Issues Lectures* so clearly demonstrates. In our view, one of the greatest challenges facing everyone in international education lies in the astonishing fact that for all our world-minded ecumenical zeal, most of us know precious little about what others also interested in international education are doing. We need a major strategic effort among ourselves to reexamine what we are doing, why we are doing it, and, especially, how we can work more closely and effectively in the great task of international education.

A FORMAL INTERNATIONAL EDUCATION

For those of us addressing international education from within academic institutions, the variety of definitions of the formal educational problem provides even further difficulties in determining the course we should take in addressing it. The problem is seen by some as a simple lack of knowledge about other peoples, cultures, and governments. Others see the difficulty as one of there being an inability on the part of Americans to deal with the complexity of the international system. Still others see the problem as being one of a lack of understanding of or sympathy for other cultures and the motivations that underlie their actions in both domestic and international politics.

Foreign policy decision-makers in the United States often disregard public opinion on international matters with an argument that the public knows little of such affairs and cannot be relied on to provide useful advice or guidance. Policy-makers are primarily concerned with the public's lack of awareness of basic facts about international affairs. For those of us whose concern is with the public's involvement in the policy-making process, the informational problem is critical. Lack of awareness on international problems will mean little public input and less governmental responsibility to constituent interests in the international arena. The lack of knowledge is followed by a lack of participation. This is, unfortunately, a common problem in the United States.

We cannot ignore the other facets of knowledge in discussing approaches to international education, however. Factual information without the analytical capability to provide a context for the facts will do little to advance the public's role in international affairs. Lack of understanding will similarly result in an insensitive application of knowledge that may ultimately be counterproductive. International education cannot ignore one of the elements of knowledge without having sometimes severe consequences for the others and for the role of the public being educated for a participatory and democratic foreign policy.

HOW GOOD HAS OUR INTERNATIONAL EDUCATION BEEN?

The most easily identifiable form of knowledge is the factual. It is most readily tested ("What is the capital of Bolivia?") and the most easily taught and learned. We have commonly used the factual knowledge indicator in assessments of all education about what is going on in the international realm. If we accept factual knowledge as the most easily obtainable form of knowledge, reflections on it may also say something about the levels of knowledge in the more difficult areas.

In the late 1930s, as tension increased in Europe, a number of studies were conducted that asked the public if they were familiar with events that had been well covered by the newspapers at that time. The polls generally indicated a lack of familiarity with contemporary international relations among the general public, as had always been suspected. In spring of 1939, for example, only 35 percent of a national sample were familiar with the Italian invasion of Albania. After the war, public knowledge remained astonishingly low. A 1946 survey asked six knowledge questions about international affairs. Only 8 percent of the public were able to identify all six of the answers; 16 percent knew none of them; 62 percent knew only three or fewer. Other studies showed that this lack of knowledge was a consistent attribute of the general public.

In 1979, the President's Commission on Foreign Language and International Studies concluded that there had been "a serious deterioration in this country's language and research capacity, at a time when an increasingly hazardous international military, political and economic environment is making unprecedented demands on America's resources, intellectual capacity and public sensitivity." The President's Commission was primarily an assemblage of expert opinion. Their view was buttressed by empirical studies.

In 1980, a study on the public's knowledge about Asia was conducted on a nationwide basis in the United States. The results of the very extensive study led the author to conclude that "The picture that emerges from all these responses is most disquieting."[1] Less than one-third of the respondents regarded Japan as a democratic nation and at least one-tenth thought that the governments of Singapore, South Korea, and Thailand were communist. Other misconceptions were found to be embarrassingly numerous.

Although most public opinion polls do not contain questions that test knowledge about foreign affairs, an ABC–*Washington Post* poll, conducted in October of 1981, did ask two knowledge questions. The poll contacted 1505 randomly selected respondents throughout the country by phone. One of the knowledge questions asked if the respondent knew whether the United States or the Soviet Union was a member of NATO. Only 47 percent of the respondents knew that the United States was the NATO member. The other question asked whether the respondent knew which two nations were involved in the SALT talks. Only 37 percent correctly identified them as the United States and the Soviet Union. On critical issues involving the United States, even relatively elementary questions cannot be answered correctly by a substantial portion of the American public.

Both the impressions of experts and scholars and the results of systematic nationwide polls confirm that the public is not knowledgeable on international matters. When factual knowledge is poor, we must suspect that analytical understanding and cross-cultural understanding are at similar or even lower levels.

Public officials and foreign policy decision-makers are aware of this deficiency and often disregard public input in acting for the nation as a whole. In critical times, in a very interdependent world, American democratic institutions are faltering for want of a better understanding on the part of all Americans of what exists and what is happening beyond our borders.

---

[1]William Watts, *Americans Look at Asia: A Need for Understanding* (Washington: Potomac Associates, 1980), p. 17.

AN AGENDA FOR A BETTER INTERNATIONAL EDUCATION

There is no course that one can offer or take that will result in an immediate increase in understanding of what is going on in the world around us. The remedy lies in a shift of emphasis in the entire educational system, elementary schools through universities, and in a socialization of Americans no longer in the schools so that circumstances and events in El Salvador or Malaysia are seen to be as important to us as those in our local communities or our nation's capital. There are, therefore, two domains in which action needs to be taken: the curricula of the schools and universities and the informal education that reaches both children and adults through media other than those of the classroom.

There is room for expansion of international education in all of its manifestations. It is particularly important in the United States, with its extensive and deeply penetrating involvement throughout the world, for the broadest possible base of the citizenry to be aware of international events, their context, and their impact on the United States. It is around this theme of educating the citizenry of a democratic system heavily involved in international affairs that we have organizeed the ITT Key Issues Lecture Series and this volume.

We wish to thank Dr. Stanley Heginbotham, chief of the Foreign Affairs and National Defense Division, Congressional Research Service at the Library of Congress; Dr. Sherry Mueller Norton, director of International Programs for the Institute of International Education; Samuel DePalma, former director of international relations for the ITT Corporation; Drs. Duncan L. Clarke and Jack Child, our colleagues from The American University faculty; and especially Sara Hoagland, a Ph.D. candidate in international relations here. All devoted a great deal of time and effort to preparing introductions for our distinguished group of speakers and were instrumental in making them feel welcome.

We would be remiss if we did not express personal appreciation to Mrs. Mary Eager, who handled all of the physical arrangements for the lectures; to Mrs. Ernestine Taylor and Patrick Garvey, who helped prepare this volume for publication; and to Susana Howell, whose editorial contributions were invaluable.

ONE

Rethinking International Education

Richard T. Arndt

Richard T. Arndt, at the time of this lecture, was the senior advisor, Bureau of Educational and Cultural Affairs, at the United States Information Agency. Prior to joining the USIA in 1961, Dr. Arndt was assistant professor of French literature and humanities at Columbia University. He has served as cultural attaché at U.S. embassies in Beirut, Colombo, Tehran, Rome, and Paris. From 1972 to 1974, he served as deputy director for Latin American programs and director of the Office of Youth, Student and Special Programs, at the Department of State. He later served as director of policy, planning, and evaluation at USIA, and now is coordinator for educational and cultural affairs for the Office of Near Eastern, South Asian, and North African Affairs of USIA.

INTRODUCTION

At least four honors attach to my presentation in this book. First, there is the honor of opening this prestigious series, targeted to the key issues of our time, in this case, the "unfinished agenda" of international education, or "IE" as we affectionately call it. Second, there is honor because this event provides a superb example of a unique American habit, that collaboration between enlightened corporate leadership and the public-spirited, policy-relevant universities that so distinguish our American style. Third, you have invited a Foreign

1

Service officer to initiate a discussion on the sacred turf of the Title VI empire, so long under the enlightened sponsorship of the Department of Education and its friends in the university world of language and area studies. Fourth, you honor diplomacy and, more specifically, cultural diplomacy by giving attention to a member of a once happy breed, which today may stand near the brink of extinction. On behalf of my cultural attaché colleagues past and present, rarely consulted and certainly never allowed to ramble on for forty minutes, I thank you.

Whatever international education is or means, cultural diplomats are chief among its front-line servants. Yet we are rarely involved in the planning. Ambassador George Kennan knew this when he wrote, to one of us, this poignant sentence: "I know of no profession which must more sorely try the souls of its practitioners than yours." Ambassador Kennan, one of the most cultured and cultural of American diplomats, knows us well. Were he here, he might warn you that my colleagues and I, with our weary souls, sometimes project a certain amount of confusion when we try to generalize from experience. There are three dangers.

The first we may call the Rip Van Winkle effect. Diplomats live abroad for long periods of time, say ten years at a stretch, with only short visits home. And cultural diplomats live abroad with a special kind of intensity that may disorient them to American life on return. The more profoundly we sink into another culture in order to understand it, and that after all is our job, the greater the risk of losing sight of home base. Some uncharitable souls, indeed, accuse us of naiveté, dupery, and even cowardice, of surrendering to the enemy in the "war of ideas." We prefer to believe we follow Spinoza in trying to understand. Yet, like Rip returned from his long sleep, we do carry doubtful virtues. Whatever we may have learned and experienced abroad, we are correspondingly out of touch with the fabric of day-to-day life in America—some books, some news items, some pennant races, some intellectual controversies, some TV specials, some films we shall never know. In my case, I have yet to catch up on fifteen years of "M*A*S*H." Still, we may take some small comfort from our less cluttered memories, which permit us in some respects to see things more clearly, from the perspective afforded by distance in time and space. This permits comparative judgments, sometimes disconcerting ones. This characteristic makes us uneasy company, all in all, and our friends wisely treat us with marked distrust.

A second flaw inheres in the phrase "scholar-bureaucrat," often applied or misapplied to us. In the hyphen, there resides a world of ambiguity. Scholars, after all, are taught to ask questions, to keep an open mind, literally to play with ideas, knocking disparate thoughts about in new contexts so as to bring forth new questions and thus new light. Scholars use wit and irony; they learn from Montaigne to doubt all statements and from Machiavelli to distrust the motivations behind them. For scholars, thought takes time and time is in ample supply. Bureaucrats, on the other hand, avoid questions. They learn to have opinions, or "policies," at the ready. They know how to back them with the facts that come to hand in the available time. Wit and irony, based on imagination, are out. Play, in a carefully counted forty-hour week, is noted as sick leave. Skepticism may be appropriate when dealing with subordinates, but supervisors see doubt as weakness or negative thinking. Put these conflicting views of the world into one person and each can compound the other's weaknesses: the scholar's questions confuse the bureaucrat; the bureaucrat lacks time and staff to answer them; the scholar's anxiety at what he does not know mounts higher. This relentless cycle can scramble good brains in no time at all. In short, to be a scholar-bureaucrat is probably impossible, and to be accused of being one most often means you are neither.

My friend E. A. Bayne once reminded me of a third problem facing cultural diplomats, even when they dwell exclusively among other diplomas. A diplomat by training is an advocate. His job is to promote the national interest in a fairly uncertain field, that of international law and foreign relations. But a cultural attaché's functions lie closer to those of a teacher. In one way or another, we invest our time and resources in educational acts which, certainly over time and possibly in the short run as well, can promote national interests.

Yet a teacher cannot lie, or at least must not seem to. Sisela Bok has reminded us of the myriad sly forms which lying can take, and one of our great American diplomats left us his memoirs under the title *Lying in State*. Given the choice between one of the many forms of lying in the short run and maintaining a reputation for the honesty and, yes, scholarship which in the long run will make his words credible and therefore persuasive, the cultural diplomat prefers the truth.

That task, choosing the truth, can indeed try the soul. As for my presentation here tonight, I shall not quote a recent President and promise never to lie. That would be presumptuous, given the difficulty of ever achieving anything so simple as the truth. But I can say I shall not lie consciously.

With these apologies, I plan tonight to mix the scholar's questions with the bureaucrat's assertions and swirl them around in the style of the teacher. The cocktail will have a mildly outrageous quality, I suspect, and should provoke dissent; at least I hope so.

Part of my madness is methodical: I would like to awaken interest in a field of study, one neglected by researchers. Anywhere from six to ten million Americans have lived abroad during the last three decades; yet I am ever amazed that journalists, scholars, filmmakers, critics, and novelists only rarely attack the meaning of that significant fact. Not that the absence of such study seems to have made much difference for our national understanding or nonunderstanding of international affairs.

Yet there are unique questions raised by the choice of millions to live abroad, by their presence and impact, by the impact of other cultures on our lives as Americans and on American life, by the perceptions others have of us, by those we have of them. I plan, therefore, as responsibly and as creatively as I can, to provoke your interest and the attention of others who may someday focus thought and research on the meaning of America's experience abroad.

One last apology: my style will be informal. With apologies to Denis Diderot and Michel Foucault, this is *not* a lecture. More a *causerie* perhaps, a chat with some friends about common concerns. I know of no other way to justify the unbuttoned kind of thinking I propose to inflict upon you this evening.

THE PARADOXES OF INTERNATIONAL EDUCATION

Seldom has a marriage been more solid or lasting than that between the two words in the phrase "international education," the pretext for this evening's thoughts. Every American surely assumes knowledge of what IE means. Some know a little about its explicit history of almost sixty years and its implicit history extending back at least as far as the ancient Greeks. But try to translate the phrase into a variety of foreign languages, including British English, and it slips through the fingers. So my first question: *do* we know what we mean? In the United States of the 1980s, is the phrase as clear as we would like to think?'

For members of the International Studies Association, whose annual meetings generally include a dozen or so panels on the subject of IE, it is appropriate to speak of an agenda. But in our beloved American system—or well-organized nonsystem—is there any way even to construct such an agenda? Agendas imply orderly meetings with rules of order and expectations of action. With international education in America today, I fear we are closer to a kind of pep rally: we have a few cheerleaders and a passable crowd rooting for an underequipped team involved in an undetermined sport and competing against an unspecified opponent at some moment in the future.

I am sufficiently convinced we are not always clear on our meanings to have entitled these thoughts a "rethinking." First, I want to examine with you some of the meanings and nonmeanings of "international education" in the light of American cultural and historical factors. Then I want to suggest some ways of adding neglected dimensions, and of focusing the idea and dividing it into manageable pieces, while warning of various traps that lie along the way. If we can then agree on definitions and on how to think about IE, perhaps we can agree on ways of establishing some informal national priorities and principles, in ways appropriate to our national style.

History, as ever, is our context. Indeed, we must venture into the even darker jungles of cultural history. Let us begin with the word "international."

The title of Michael Kammen's brilliant *People of Paradox* reminds us that our nation was born in a state of ambivalence about the rest of the world, and it has remained so. All nations are ambivalent about other nations, but the United States was designed that way. We had to reject Europe if we were to begin to define our own identity. Jefferson, living amidst his homegrown inventions and his imported European cultural treasures, warned us more than once about the temptations of Europe. Despite its cultural wealth, Europe and its politics represented all that was to be feared. Outside Europe, in the eighteenth century equivalent of the Third World, there were other lands. These Americans treated either as land to be conquered and settled, like our frontiers; as territory to be liberated from European domination and kept free for our own purposes, like Latin America; or as territory to be relegated to *exotica*, hence to explorers and scholars, and thus ignored.

Our foreign policy, as Arthur Schlesinger recently observed, has steered a careful course between geopolitical, balance-of-powers, nationalist realism and the idealistic rhetoric of one version or another of making the world safe for democracy (our kind of course). Some of us worried from the outset about the social and economic development, and the souls, of selected less-fortunate foreign brethren; others of us drove the hard bargains of the Yankee trader.

American isolationism, given new importance and form after Theodore Roosevelt discovered the subtle joys of international meddling, posed its own paradox: isolationism drew both on the ignorance of the know-nothings and the sophistication of the experts who feared the curse of too-rapid modernization in traditional societies. We Americans are proud to be considered practical idealists, and we live comfortably with that self-image. Yet the phrase is a contradiction, expressing the paradox of American power and lying deep down in the idea of IE.

In cultural terms as well, we have been persistently ambivalent about non-American cultures, and this from the beginning. Other cultures, primarily Europe, first seemed to threaten our efforts to become American. Later, waves of lesser-European and non-European immigrants would pose a different kind of cultural threat. Only recently could we turn our immigrant origins toward fueling an ingenious search for ethnic identity in the context of a pluralist nation. Only in recent years have we endeavored to celebrate rather than persecute difference.

As Americans, we sought our identity in action, in *our* actions, thus in the here and now, and our philosophers devised a pragmatic style to justify our ways to God. As the "here" reflects our disinterest in geography, in the elsewhere, so the "now" reveals our distrust of history, whose role in locating America in the unfolding of world civilization has still too little value to assure it a central place in American curricula. Even when we did restore it, at certain universities, for example, dressed in the priestly garb of "Western Civ," we tended to forget the non-Western roots and tributaries of America.

In cultural terms, are Americans more ambivalent about other nations than the citizens of the rest of the world? Perhaps not so very much, in truth; but in our open and pluralist society, it is more visible. Most nations leave foreign affairs to a tiny elite and allow the natural hostilities toward other countries and cultures to play freely through national attitudes; in countries like these, only diplomats need international education. Americans on the other hand, suspect foreign relations are too important to leave to diplomats; besides, we depend upon an informed public to feed our democratic process. So we turn, in our natural American way, to the educational community for help in informing our people, in broadening access to and participation in foreign policy. IE is a partial response to that need; yet one wonders if it has reduced our national confusion.

In social and political terms, Americans *are* better aware of our paradoxes. We celebrate the individual against the state; we defend the autonomy of the press and the university, leaving both, along with public transporation and most communications, to the tough mercies of the private sector. No tenets of American life are more religiously defended, even when these vital institutions suffer from malnutrition, than free enterprise and individualism. Yet abroad we pass for conformists. Seen from Europe, our politics produce two consensus parties, barely distinguishable in ideology and adaptable in program proportionately to the nearness of elections. In foreign affairs, our parties confound overseas observers by concentrating almost exclusively on domestic issues. What is more parochial than an American political party? What is more provincial than our assumption that all elections will turn solely on the state of the economy come October? We are, as a nation, ill equipped to understand foreign politics, and foreigners have equal trouble with ours. The difference is that *we*, as a nation, do not seem to mind not understanding. "International" then is defined in part by the history of our nation and by our value structure, hence by our paradoxes. If the contradictions bother us less than they do our French friends, they nonetheless make it harder for us to know what we are talking about in IE.

Alas, when we come to "education," it is just as difficult. In the land of the self-made, education was long in acquiring the kind of value that most other countries gave it. Universities at first aimed at the very few. Study was fine, if there was time, but institutional education was not needed beyond a few basic skills. When Emerson exhorted us to recognize that an American could be a scholar, to take pride in our American style, it became possible to confront our European past, to make the Grand Tour without attracting hometown gossip. The Puritan-tinged minds of a Hawthorne, of a Melville, and ultimately of a James articulated for America the deeper costs in social dislocation and spiritual confusion consequent on the discovery of our European connection, of our intellectucal and spiritual debt to our own past; and even as they did so, they found a new theme, that of the alienated artist unheeded by his audience.

Our missionaries, by the 1830s, had already begun their noble and underchronicled saga to bring Protestantism to the wretched of the earth, through the so American tools of education, especially in medicine and agriculture. Their experience reflected, even as it confirmed, the American ideal of education as mission. When the Civil War unleashed vast new industrial energies, it was relatively simple for this sense of mission to be adapted to a new mass education movement, then to spread, to expand, and to become a manifest destiny, at home and abroad.

This nineteenth century overseas educational activity, undertaken at the same time as the growth of the European colonial system, was carried out in the normally paternalistic language of the schools. The sense of American mission heightened this tone, and even while rejecting the patrician British style, we edged over into the vocabulary of empire. The educational vision of our missionaries, *mutatis mutandis*, was couched in language not unlike that of Macaulay's famous "Minute" on India's educational system as a function of administrative order.

At the same time, we were discovering at home an uncomfortable dependency on Europe. The great American universities, including the land-grant model with its unprecedented triple mission of applying knowledge as well as generating and preserving it, saw no choice but to look to Europe for their development. The federal Office of Education, from its creation, had a specific charge to draw what was required from Europe to help build our research universities. So our students began to flow to Europe, perhaps 2,000 right after the Civil War, shortly before the students of the Third World began to come to our shores—5,000 in 1911, 10,000 in 1930, and probably well over 400,000 today.

By the beginning of this century, Americans thinking about international education were poised between the giving and the getting of education, and these can be very different matters. If, as one stimulating definition suggests, imperialism is a phenomenon produced by the impact of higher-technology on lower-technology societies, then the language of the giving of education and the language of imperialism necessarily share a common vocabulary. In the getting, Americans were careful to channel European high technology democratically through our pragmatic universities into the most mundane aspects of our daily life. But in the giving, with our endless generosity and our desire to let the whole world in on our utopian secret, we paid scant attention to the way our high technology impacted on others—the marketplace could surely handle problems like justice. In the getting, we could afford to be selective, as the natural elitism of science and technology took over; but in the giving, we did what little we could, where we could, and we assumed the consequences would take care of themselves.

In the word "education," we find then an ambivalence as tortured as that in "international." Between the getting of knowledge and the giving, there is a dichotomy: humility versus a generous and gentle form of arrogance. There is as well the education training dichotomy, reflecting the European (elitist) versus the American (democratic) contrast. We find this paradox as well in the ongoing American discussion about the whole-man, the great-books, the liberal-arts, and the core-curriculum approaches, as opposed to various more implemental styles of training or skilling.

These paradoxes muddy our thinking about education and its international dimension. As an example demonstrating their power to obfuscate, a publication designed to reach concerned graduates of an Ivy League university recently commented editorially on a program to bring faculty from various in-state community colleges to its campus for a year-long seminar, as part of a commitment to help higher education in that state. Noting that the topic of this year is international education, the author writes:

We may as well inquire sheepishly, "What the hell is International Education?"

Glad you asked. It rests on the assumption—preposterous as it turns out—that one needs a special brand of knowledge in order to study foreign

*cultures. In other words the liberal education isn't enough: we must take
courses in "International Education." . . . The "International Education" malaise . . . reflects a serious lack of faith in the liberal ideal.*

I cite this text neither to dignify nor to demean it but to remind you
that confusion about the meaning of IE can have serious effects. The
confusion in these lines flows naturally from the paradox of education
in American life. It would be unwise to underestimate the sincerity of
their author, and equally unwise to assume that the meanings attrib-
uted to IE in America today are either clear, universal, or without
controversy.

A HALF-CENTURY OF GROWTH (1918–1968)

When the two words join, our prologue ends. We can leave this
breathless excursion into the labyrinths of cultural history and look at
history of a more familiar kind—that of events, and recent ones at
that.

In 1918, World War I was over. Now the world was surely safe for
democracy; the war to end all wars had been won, and we assumed a
role of leadership among nations. No one could put this historic
moment more succinctly than Fritz Stern has done:

*As history goes, American leadership is a relatively recent affliction. In
part, our global responsiblities were thrust upon us—by the weaknesses of
former allies and by the threat of new rivals. For the first century of our
national existence, we were a continental power—and even after our impe-
rial adventure in the Spanish-American War, we retained an essentially
insular outlook. Until 1917, we were blessed with the reality of privacy.
We traded with the world, we learned from it, but we were not responsible
for it. Incautiously we ditched the burden of responsibility in 1920; by
1944 it proved inescapable.*

The effects of this shift on American culture are endless. By 1918,
from every corner of the country, large numbers of Americans had for
the first time been internationally socialized by being transported to

Europe. Questions about keeping them "down on the farm, after they've seen Paree" arose all too naturally. The newfound hospitality of grateful postwar France, Italy, and Britain, and even of a resentful Germany, eased the problems encountered by American students in those countries. A generous exchange rate enabled a new generation of Americans, some of them scholars, some tourists, and some celebrants of lostness, to emulate Jefferson by touring Europe and bringing home bits, pieces, and memories of its culture.

In 1919, the marriage in America of education and internationalism was consecrated in New York City, with the founding of the Institute of International Education. IIE, brought into being by American universities and foundations, reflected the need for a national clearinghouse to coordinate the getting and giving of knowledge with regard to other nations.

Other overseas educational institutions were burgeoning. In Paris, we founded two hostels for American students and a Carnegie-sponsored home for scholars. Another endowed center in Paris, complete with swimming pool, would help students spend their leisure hours in wholesome activities. A similar healthy, near-monastic orientation kept the Fellows in the American Academy in Rome, founded twenty-odd years before but growing rapidly now with the help of J. P. Morgan, protected on their high Janiculum against the Roman fevers raging below.

At Oxford and Cambridge, visiting professorships in American studies were founded, as was a chair at the Collège de France. And the new American philanthropic foundations, restoring old monuments like Reims Cathedral and Versailles, while building new ones like the Dental Faculty of the University of Rome, created a climate without precedent for the interchange of European and American elites.

By 1930, there would be more than 5,000 American students abroad, not to mention the tourists, the business executives and the émigrés. Wilson's failure to sell Congress on the League of Nations had been political, not cultural. In cultural terms, the die was cast and the energy of the rampantly internationlist city of New York was already beginning to spill over into the rest of the nation.

In formal diplomacy, the effects were also beginning to be felt. Earlier, the indemnity paid by China for damages in the Boxer Rebellion had been allocated to educational exchange. An incident in Iran in the early 1920s would repeat this precedent. We moved from a gentleman-staffed foreign service to an institutionalized system with a corporate memory, thanks to the Rogers Act of 1925, creating the Foreign Service.

The Service would soon discover, as the French had done long before, the cultural dimensions of diplomacy. The French did not establish a separate overseas cultural service until the 1920s; the British Council was not founded until 1935, in response to Nazi propaganda programs.

In the United States it was not until 1938 that the State Department yielded to the obvious (with the extreme reluctance natural to any federal agency—above all, one staffed by an educated elite). Urged by the universities, the foundations, and IIE, State agreed to provide an office for the benign coordination of overseas educational and cultural activities. The period from 1938 to 1950, so ably documented and analyzed by Frank Ninkovich in his remarkable *Ideas of Diplomacy*, would see this office led out of its passive role into activist programs by the wartime energy of the young Nelson Rockefeller, who believed with the British that a dynamic cultural program was an important weapon for countering the Axis threat, especially in Latin America.

If the First World War began the international socialization of Americans, the Second carried it farther: more Americans went abroad, and they went to many more countries; expanded media coverage, not to mention the newly powerful Hollywood machine, brought the War close to every American. Afterwards, Americans like Senator William Fulbright, Rhodes Scholar in the 1930s, approached the postwar period with a new sophistication flowing from close observation of the history of the twenties and thirties.

Some kind of United Nations was taken for granted and so, later, was UNESCO—perhaps too much so, as it now seems. The Marshall Plan, pouring into Europe an average of $3 billion annually and thousands of Americans, was an amazing sucess, even if it left its share of illusions about the power of money, good intentions, and technical assistance. The parallel success of German and Japanese reeducation fed other illusions about quick fixes.

Yet our illusions were more sophisticated than those of the 1920s. Who in the late 1940s believed that *this* war had ended them all, or that the world was safe for democracy? The war drums of its colder cousin could already be heard, and there was thunder in China. So it was perhaps natural that the newly dynamized government cultural programs, now wedded to the foreign affairs interests of the United States, should *not* revert to prewar benignity but carry their new-found vigor into the Cold War era. Because the sense of mission does not easily die in America, the history of the early postwar period is naturally strewn with the language of the Crusades. Americans of the 1940s and 1950s were still idealists, however sophisticated.

In 1953, from the land of Machiavelli, Luigi Barzini felt strongly enough to warn us against our idealism and against simplistic solutions:

> *How can Americans quickly adapt themselves to the permanent war, which has to be prepared, threatened, feared or fought, hot or cold, every day of their future life? . . . The temptation is always with them to rush into whatever there is to be done, do it, and get it over with. Who will tell them that the flames will never be extinguished and they will never go to bed?*

Brash young America knew better than to heed this kind of tired old European cynicism. We scoffed too at Europe's insistent stress on the effect on us of our Puritan ancestors. A recent and typical definition by Professor Heikko Oberman of Tübingen University provides a perfect example of Europe's perception of the dangers of unacknowledged American Puritanism. He asks:

> *To what extent did the American enlightenment, somewhat different from the French, combine secular knowledge with religious obligation to form a "civic religion" unknown in Europe? Was there a genuine American Puritanism whose concept of freedom, coupled with a missionary mentality, produced its own value hierarchy and urged the assumption of supranational responsibility for spreading freedom to the rest of the world?*

Whether the American mission was focused on heathens or hunger, Nazis or Communists, it still looked like a mission to friendly neutral observers. Justifiable or not, our idealism and sense of mission are part of what makes us unique as Americans.

The War brought education into international politics and into proximity with programs in information and propaganda, both of the white and black varieties. At the end of the War, we found three symbolic actors: General Donovan and his OSS, Elmer Davis and his OWI, Archibald MacLeish and his cultural programs. These three forces would ultimately regroup and form the CIA on the one hand and USIA (with State's CU) on the other, and the USIA configuration would persist, with various reforms and reshapings, until today.

International education entered two decades of stunning growth after the War, escaping from the context of the federal diplomats. The GI Bill allowed veterans to stay on in Europe, many for study. The Marshall Plan and German and Japanese reeducation had important training dimensions at home and abroad. The Fulbright Act of 1946, an ingenious way of settling war debts without disrupting national economies, opened a new era of exchanges, turning rusty swords into scholarships.

The Smith-Mundt Act of 1948 broadened the program's authority and provided dollar allocations. First-generation Fulbright returnees multiplied the investment as they concocted hundreds of year-abroad programs, which even today sponsor perhaps 10,000 American students annually in France and Italy alone. And in the 1940s and 1950s, programs like the student exchanges of the American Field Service and the Experiment in International Living began their growth.

In 1957, shocked by the Soviet ability to launch a basketball-sized satellite, Congress passed the National Defense Education Act, authorizing among other things federal funding for university foreign language and area studies programs, and bringing the U.S. Office of Education into the game. The great foundations, ever out front, expanded their own important commitment to international education. In 1961, the Third World became part of the curriculum when the Peace Corps attacked three separate purposes: helping others, shaping the American image abroad, and informing Americans about the world. Later in 1961, an expanded Fulbright-Hays Act was passed. The International Baccalaureate, in the 1960s, began its efforts to produce uniform international secondary school–leaving criteria, a major step toward free educational interchange.

The apex, or was it the nadir, was the Internatonal Education Act of 1966, which as every schoolboy knows never received a penny of appropriated funds. Extending the motto of the University of Wisconsin, where education reaches the boundaries of the state, proclaiming that the responsibilities of American education covered the entire globe, this noble document fell flat. Its demise marked the end of an era of burgeoning. It was the first early warning of trouble for IE.

TWO DECADES OF BOOM

Let us look at this vibrant twenty-year period in the aftermath of World War II, a period in which international education took shape as a concept and boomed as a program. I offer a few descriptive thoughts, listed almost as they come to mind and without pretense of their being a complete description of this complex period:

• The numbers were large: it is not inaccurate to speak of a proliferation. No nation ever exported and imported, before or since, so many students, researchers, and teachers, in absolute terms.

• There was little or no central coordination, no attention to aggregate numbers. A thousand flowers bloomed. Soon a country like France, in which higher education is a function of the State, began to wonder why thousands of Americans should fill scarce places in its universities at no cost when French students in the United States paid heavy tuition fees. And Pakistan began to worry about the deculturation and deracination of their young people during the deeply emotional, family-based experience of the American Field Service year.

• Most of these exchanges took place in a private-sector American framework that foreign governments found impossible to match and hard to deal with. It was difficult for Americans, used to moving easily from Kansas to California, to understand why foreign nations seemed so stodgy, bureaucratic, and frustrating. Important political and economic niceties, to Americans, seemed to reflect foreign orneriness, incompetence, and occasional malice.

• The tone, the vocabulary, and the style of this expansion, conscious or not, had a hegemonic tinge to it, lodged in the persistent notion of education as a mission. Few Americans ever dreamed of ruling the world, but accusations of cultural imperialism, not only from the predictable enemies, dupes, and disinformed but from sensitive friends, began to be heard.

• Responsiblity for IE, during these years, was dispersed through several federal agencies with only the merest coordinative structure between them. Charles Frankel counted fifteen separate agencies with interests in overseas educational and research relationships.

• Total government investment, all considered, was small. The real quantitative impact came from the ignition of private energies, including of course the universities. At its high point, the budget for the Department of State's Bureau of Educational and Cultural Affairs barely edged over $50 million, while the Office of Education struggled hard to get its budget up to $20 million.

• Many of the important funding breakthroughs in Congress were dressed in the language of the military: Fulbright was funded by surplus military sales, for peace we needed a Corps, education legislation was geared to National Defense. When he heard the NDEA was to be renamed without the word "Defense," one university areas studies figure exclaimed, "My God! Now we'll *never* get any money!"

• While the products of exchange produced a mountain of publications and reports, the process itself generated little serious research and analysis. What did appear, as Ninkovich notes, was a "somewhat anemic and inbred literature." Meanwhile, federal administrators, trying to make the most out of too little, skimped on research and evalutation.

• The dynamic style of many federal education programs overseas, particularly those with their home in USIA, persisted. It was deemed unthinkable to go back to the benign and coordinative prewar style. Programs defined as part of our foreign affairs support system tended to become ends in themselves rather than links in a process. And universities learned they could live with this concept.

• There was real progress in lauguage and area studies, but as Harlan Cleveland would point out in 1980, the area studies programs were surprisingly insular, separate from the rest of their universities. One typical pattern, an outwardly expanding language program, often incurred stern oppostion from social scientists and historians.

These are snippets, thrown out at random for historians to peruse, but there is much more to say about this era.

It is useful to note that exchanges took place for different purposes during these years. One way to categorize them starts from the different kinds of bilateral relationships. In terms of what Americans and foreigners expected from each other, there were perhaps three kinds of distinct exchange relationships: getting, giving, and confronting. With Europe, we were still in a predominantly getting stage. European universities were still too proud to admit their need, and Americans tended to look up to Europe's history of humanism.   ⟶

⤳ Even a field of acknowledged United States expertise like American studies or American literature found hard going in Europe, if only because of the politics of university appointments and budgets. Today it is still nearly impossible for an American to hold a tenured position in a European university, while Europeans teach in America, where we admit our need, by the thousands. The second category of bilateral relationships, based on giving, takes place with the developing countries. Here we are not students but teachers, and their students come to the United States to get what they cannot get at home. A third group is typified by the Soviet-bloc countries, where the mode is confrontational, the style wary and exploratory. The purposes are tentative and partial, the tone suspicious, the product highly limited.

This typology admits too many exceptions to be very useful, but it reminds us once again that international education means several things. Aside from the highly politicized Soviet relationship and the very different program with China, we are still poised between giving and getting. Each bilateral relationship has its own history and character, but by and large each is still either a giving or a getting process, each covering a subtle mirror-play of national pride and ambivalence.

Surprisingly, with an investment of national resources on this scale, there was little attention in the postwar period given to how these international graduates would be utilized and how their impact could be maximized, whether in our educational systems, in business, or in government. The need to equip ourselves for a role as world leader was obvious, yet we did nothing to ensure the best use of the human resources we trained. Planning and directive thinking do not happen easily in a country where market forces and free enterprise form part of our religion. In sharp contrast, democratic Norway, which in 1945 recognized that its universities were inadequate to the needs of the modern world, systematically set about using every available bilateral and multilateral relationship to feed a thirty-year plan for university development, a more methodical version of what the United States had done in the nineteenth century with the creation of the Office of

Education. In the 1950s, some American states like California set up coherent plans for the statewide articulation of higher education, but Americans would never dream of channeling a system's graduates into specific job markets. We are a long way even today from getting our national money's worth from investments in international education.

The absence of a mechanism for broad indicative planning poses obvious questions. Did government foreign affairs agencies canvass returned Fulbrighters and later Peace Corp veterans? Were the products of government-backed area studies programs exploited so as to bring new sophistication into our foreign affairs research capability and into the practice of diplomacy? Why did the important investments of the 1950s in early language education and new languages in the universities crumble in the 1960s? Why did business not see that trained and cosmopolitan young people were part of its future? Why was a national need, defined so clearly in the 1950s, handled with so little conceptual infrastructure, follow-up, and continuity?

These first two postwar decades, then, were marked by proliferation and abundance, but by little coordination, planning, or evaluation, by an indifference to international political niceties which was already causing nascent bilateral irritations, by persistent cultural ambivalence, by an implicit and ever-subtle kind of hegemonic utopianism, by an absence of personnel utilization strategies, by a failure to institutionalize gains, and by scant guidelines on how private and public funds might work together.

By 1945 it was obvious that the role of world leader, whether or not we wanted it, was ours. Surely it was not much later that we began to realize that international leadership brought with it a growing interdependence on the kind Henry Kissinger was to articulate at the end of the 1960s. There is little evidence of a national policy consensus during these two postwar decades, little to indicate that our nation knew that educational preparation for life in a newly interdependent world was closely related to survival.

THE LESSONS OF DECLINE

To aggregate the twenty-year period between the War and the failure of IEA, even in so random a way, is to conceal one of its most interesting characteristics, the gradual emergence of the idea of globalizing international education. We are not surprised, in the postwar period, to see programs designed (even in a unplanned economy) to build competence and professionalism, for example, in foreign affairs—hence the rise of international relations programs in our universities. Nor are we surprised that American universities see it as their duty to welcome foreign students. What is unusual, though perfectly consonant with the spirit of mission of American education, is the growing awareness and articulation, even in the hermetic climate of legislative mandates, of two other aspects of IE: the need to educate Americans *generally* about foreign cultures and nations, and a sense of American educational commitment to educate the rest of the world.

The Fulbright-Hays Act of 1961 captures the spirit of these years. Its statement of purpose outlines four goals and three lines of action. First, it proposes "to increase mutual understanding between the *people* of the United States and the *people* of other countries" (my stress: the people, not the elites, the influentials, or the leaders) and to do this through exchanges. Second, it proposes to *strengthen* the ties which *unite* us to other nations (my stress: acceptance of interdependence). Third, it proposes to promote international cooperation for educational and cultural advancement, presumably by support to UNESCO. And fourth, in summary, it proposes to aim for international relations that are "friendly, sympathetic and peaceful." In the context of the legislative rhetorician's art, this is an impressive statement. It is significant that no mention of foreign policy goals occurs in this text, though the idea had been made explicit in the Smith-Mundt legislation thirteen years earlier.

Another surprise attaches to the means allotted to the second goal. The Act will strengthen our ties to others (again, my stress):

> . . . *by demonstrating the educational and cultural interests, developments, and achievements of the United States* and other nations, *and the contributions being made toward a peaceful and more fruitful life for people throughout the world.*

Assuming that this prose is no accident and that an ever-wise Congress meant what it said, we see embodied here the idea that Americans need help in understanding others. At the same time we bear an educational responsibility to others. This language, contiguous in time with the Peace Corps' third goal, and later to trigger USIA's "Second Mandate," builds on a time-honored goal of American education. This is the idea that would blossom into the ill-fated flower of the International Education Act.

From this period another monument remains, of the most permanent kind: bureaucratic structure. Rather than create an agency or expand an existing structure to administer the Fulbright-Hays Act, it seemed natural to parcel out the programs to existing bodies: State Department, USIA, AID, the Office of Education, and several lesser players. What Congress had put together, Congress allowed to be rendered asunder by executive decision. The gerrymandering of this act, done surely without malice and in the cool spirit of political realism, divided major responsibilities for IE between four principal agencies, each defined by its own criteria, purposes, mandates, and self-image.

AID took what could be comprised under then-current definitions of technical assistance. The Office of Education took charge of building the strength, in the tradition of its NDEA Title VI programs, of American university language and area studies programs. The State Department's Bureau of Educational and Cultural Affairs handled the Fulbright Program and all exchange elements, including some minimal responsibility for foreign students in the United States. USIA was given responsibility for "telling America's story" through books, libraries, English teaching, visual arts, and various other elements.

There can be no doubt that the parceling out of this act watered down its impact. Washington turf wars and jurisdictional disputes, not to mention cutthroat budget games, subtracted predictably from what Congress's language seems to have intended. For those of us interested in defining the American meaning of IE in practical terms, it meant, for example, that the projection of American values overseas through educational exchanges was handled separately from the enrichment of the American learning experience, or that foreign students in the United States might study under the auspices of three different agencies, each with its own purposes and terms. No coordinating committees or interdepartmental groups, however vigorous and well-intentioned, could put this Humpty back together.

How can we explain the sharp reverses of 1967–1968? The story of the abundance of the two postwar decades is not complete without a look at its attendant collapse. The nonfunding of the IEA was the first sign. Then funding for the State's Department's Bureau of Educational and Cultural Affairs declined over two years by almost 50 percent. Meanwhile, in the private sector, the great foundations began at almost the same time to pare, then to slash the size of their international commitments.

Historians may someday focus on the reasons for this generalized retreat, at the same time, across such a broad front. Charles Frankel, a key participant, found sufficient explanation in an increasing Washington preoccupation with the Vietnam War. Others have suggested that interagency rivalries and turf battles, perhaps exacerbated by budget drains to Vietnam, were major contributors. Some see backlash against universities and intellecutuals critical of United States action in Vietnam. Some believe that central figures in Congress like the famous John Rooney, again perhaps prompted by Vietnam, saw an overcommitment that needed to be brought into focus. Others point the finger at dwellers of one office or another of the White House. Still others see rising domestic priorities in education crowding out international activities, a reflecton of the elitist discussion.

Did anyone notice a leftward movement among the American returnees from overseas education? Some suggest, one hopes facetiously, that the IEA failed because it had no military language in its title. Equally facetious is the idea that, after putting a man on the moon, America's problems were perceived to disappear. Some argue that the effectiveness of exchanges, the buildingblocks of international education, had never been proven by appropriate research and evaluative mechanisms. Other see the beginnings of a crisis in national values, one that will persist at least into the 1980s as the precarious idealist-realist balance of the 1940s, 1950s, and 1960s begins to give way to a more realist-nationalist stance.

Whether the end of the IE boom reflected a new mood in America, bureaucratic ineptness, competing priorities, or personal malice—this remains to be sorted out. One suspects that, like most turning points in history, it was a little of all of these, and a lot more as well.

WHERE ARE WE?

It is time to relinquish history, for we have arrived at our own decade. As historians love to remind us, the present is not their period.

But it is ours, and it is time to look at the present, hopefully with renewed perceptions from our jaunt throught time.

Let us return to our friend Rip Van Winkle, after his adjustable sleep, this time of roughly forty-five years. Ask him if he sees any progress today regarding the internationalization of American life. On the positive side, Rip would surely find an astonishing number of strong private programs with steadily growing alumni bodies: every year that the American Field Service, Fulbright program, or the Johns Hopkins branch in Bologna survives, the body of internationalized American and foreign alumni and friends grows. He would find perhaps ten million other Americans who have lived abroad.

He would find a great number of Americans who can handle foreign languages, some at extremely high levels of competency and not merely in the languages of Western Europe (true, he would also find some of these high-quality American linguists working in restuarants and driving taxis). He would find rich new opportunities in the unprecedented numbers of educated immigrants, refugees, and temporary residents mixed into American life, not to mention foreign students. He would find, in the public media and especially television, a new foreign language sophistication: we see films and news from all over the world; opera (albeit with subtitles) graces our television; our films are polyglot when appropriate.

Those who see TV commercials as profound insights into our values will note the use of Italian in promoting wines; others will remember that curious American folk hero, the man who liked the electric razor so much he bought the company, and wonder what values pressed him to broadcast the same commercial to an American audience, with our hero speaking fluent, undubbed Japanese.

He would find new American appreciation of ethnicity: he might meet Italian-Americans who had changed their Anglicized names back to the original, for example. In the Congress, after the rejection of the attempted 1981 cut in the Fulbright Program, he would have noted a newfound realization that exchanges matter. He would find courses in international relations in every university in the land. He would find area studies programs in European and non-European languages built into university structures across the country, however precariously. He would everywhere find innovative programs, like The American University's new program in development management, or Georgetown's joint program in foreign service and linguistics, to take two examples.

He would find corporate sensitivity, the kind epitomized by ITT's ten-year scholarship effort, by Mobil's full-page magazine ad for the American Field Service, or by the Ad Council's nationwide campaign in support of youth exchanges. He would find an astonishing range of imports, from cars to television sets, and the most internationalized food industry in the world.

All over the land, he would find experimental people-networks trying to foster better international relations and to guide the internationalization of their state's curricula. He would admire the patient work of organizations like the World Affairs Council and Global Perspectives. At an annual meeting of the International Studies Association, he would find a dozen or more events devoted to IE. He would find federal budgets at unprecedented levels, even if constant-dollar calculations look less optimistic. He would find mounds of books, ephemeral publications, periodicals, reports, studies, and manifests devoted to foreign affairs and the study of foreign cultures. Rip would be impressed.

It surprises even veteran practitioners of international education to hear it added up this way. We who daily put ourselves into the painful step-by-step work of it do not always remember where we were not so many years ago. We do not always remember that Americans have a great talent for change, perhaps because, as Tocqueville wrote, "In no country in the civilized world is less attention paid to philosophy." Altogether, we have not done badly in an area where progress was not easy.

The litany of our failures is more familiar to self-critical American ears. I will not list the recent reports which point to the general decline of American secondary and even university education, to various crises in area studies and in the humanities and the social sciences, to the decline of foreign language requirements, to the Dallas students who cannot locate the United States on a world map, to an endlessly renewed sea of American provincialism about the rest of the world. Some of these indices, in the American way, are of course signs that a reaction has begun, but the list of our failures is a stern reminder of how far we have to go.

Some deeper elements might trouble our returnee from the 1930s, if we pressed him closely. He might then have to admit that, to nourish his optimism, he has used a fairly superficial set of criteria to examine a subject in which the first danger is superficiality. He might admit that many of the institutions he cites rest on a fairly fragile base. He might note that, under the last two administrations, there has been a serious erosion of the notion of professionalism in public life, specifically so in foreign affairs. He might worry that the continuing lack of research and study into the process and value of IE makes analysis and evaluation frustrating. And he might be concerned about the presistence of isolationism, in subtle new forms.

Let me elaborate on these points, however briefly. Superficiality flows, of course, from a basic decision in our history about education. When Americans decided to broaden access to education and to educate the entire population instead of a ruling elite, it was an act of faith in the idea and capacities of education, which we trace to Jefferson. It was also a trade-off: an underinformed public opinion has impinged upon the old idea of a supersophisticated establishment. Matched person to person with counterpart international affairs leadership in Europe, Americans are very different.

I hesitate to say we are either worse or better, but we most certainly speak different cultural languages. The day has passed when European countries exchanged leaders and diplomats to whom John Adams, Jefferson, or Franklin, who knew the same Greek and Latin authors, could speak directly. American foreign affairs practitioners in our era, both political and career, have difficulty relating in any depth to their European counterparts. *Time* is not *The Economist*; the *Washington Post* is neither *Le Monde* nor *Die Zeit*. The gap perceived by our European friends is wider than Americans like to admit; Europe tends to give this distance an importance that Americans, when the point is raised, perceive as an attack. This gap between us must surely affect our dealings with others, perhaps more seriously than we know.

The problem of institutional fragility is apparent everywhere: whether from the effects of the recent recession, from cutbacks in the federal support system, or from the sluggish response of job markets to their products, many IE institutions report they are in trouble. There is discouragement in the area studies world; there are cutbacks in universities. Evidence that little permanent progress has been made, even after fifty years of directed therapy, mounts with each successive report or study.

The erosion of professionalism, in part at least, flows from the antigovernment rhetoric of recent years at one level and from the attack on the value of education at another. The foreign affairs community was never irresistibly attractive to the best products of internatonal education, but the effect of the new antigovernment messages has been to reduce even further the importance of the role of professionals, and this can only be a blow to IE.

Today more jobs at the upper levels go to political appointees with fewer qualifications that we have seen since the beginnings of the Foreign Service. There is no shortage of experts in this nation on Lebanon and Syria, but there is an increasing shortage of those who know how or are inclined to consult them. The endemic sluggishness of bureaucracy has always been hard to excuse, but the present alternative approach questions the very idea of professionalism and is a more serious matter. True, the foreign affairs agencies have never distinguished themselves by heavy expenditures on recruiting the best, on in-depth training and retraining, on better and more flexible utilization of trained and qualified personnel, on interchange with research centers and universities, on genuine in-depth language proficiency, or on promotion systems based on sophisticated evaluation.

Fifty years ago, there were few experts and a handful of generalists: men like Charles Bohlen and George Kennan were trained for years before they were sent to the Soviet Union. We had little, but we used it well. Today we have much and, I fear, use it little. Such trends can only discourage the universities from commitments to language and area studies and top students from dedicating their lives to foreign affairs.

It is harder to explain the continued dearth of research. The mass of literature produced by observers of IE and cultural diplomacy over the last half-century is curiously anecdotal.

There are exceptions, for example, books by Charles Frankel, Philip Coombs, Walter Johnson and Frank Colligan, Paul Simon, and others. There are continued task forces and conferences, indicating persistently that someone cares.

There was some indication, in the productions of 1980, of a newly enlightened self-criticism and realism, especially from the universities, but it was short-lived. From 1980, I would cite three examples in particular: the second IE-related edition of the *Annals*, revealingly sophisticated in contrast to its predecessor of twenty years earlier; a remarkable edition of *Change*, reporting the deliberations of the National Task Force on Education and World Learning, of the Council on Learning; and Nincovich's remarkable *Ideas of Diplomacy*, the first critical history of cultural diplomacy the country has seen.

These texts contain various frank, self-critical, and refreshing messages from the university side: Harlan Cleveland hints that area studies programs may be dangerously insular; Robert McCaughey warns that the universities cannot carry the burden of IE alone, that other channels need to be opened; Frederick Starr warns that federal support becomes a Trojan horse when it induces dependency; Wesley Posvar urges new disciplinary and interdepartmental flexibility in the universities if they are to meet these new challenges; and Nincovich analyzes as never before the ambivalences inherent in practical idealism and the contradictions inherent in the contact of culture and power. Still, these bright moments are little more than signposts, and the field remains to be explored.

The rise of a new blend of isolationist or unilateral thinking, composed of many different ingredients, need be no more than noted here. The factors involved are many and reflect the broad discussion of political values which has been underway in this land for at least a decade. Yet it is surely a factor working against the health of the internationalization of American education and life.

In sum, there is good news and bad. Despite profound negative elements, Rip Van Winkle would probably have to admit that, while serious, the situation is not entirely hopeless. Somehow we are muddling forward and perhaps even getting closer to looking hard at the deeper problems of IE. At the same time, Rip might be excused for wondering, as did the wistful title of the 1967 annual report of the State Department's Advisory Commission on Educational and Cultural Affairs: "Is Anybody Listening?"

TOWARD A DEFINITION

I promised we would *begin* with history. By now you should be wondering if we shall ever escape it. If so, I have achieved one of my purposes. We are in fact dealing with an immense and terribly complex idea, or set of ideas, inescapably linked with our history, so that it is virtually impossible to define IE in ways that will satisfy both scholar and bureaucrat; political scientist and politician; educator and newscaster; liberal and conservative; Republican and Democrat; State Department, USIA, AID, and Office of Education; NSC and CIA; European, Third Worlder, and American. I owe it to you, nevertheless, to try.

We began with the premise of interdependence. I hope it is not necessary to prove here the growing interdependency of our world. Interdependence will not go away; instead it will surely become more intense. Short of a deliberate turning back of the clock or a decision literally to withdraw from reality, we can surely agree that in social, political, economic, and technological terms the world is daily weaving a tighter web around the American Gulliver. If that is so, then I hope we can also agree that this fact places major new requirements on the American approach to education. I shall not elaborate on this basic premise.

Agreement is tougher when we focus on the role the United States should plan to play in such an interdependent world. Here value differences make discussion difficult and agreement all but impossible. One way to treat the question, however, is to jump over it. By examining two extreme versions of today's conventional wisdom on the subject, we see they lead to the same conclusion. On the one extreme, we might posit a grouping of thinkers and citizens who would have us recognize a relative decline in American power and have us focus on the need for alliance politics and the maintenance of power balances on a global scale. These we can loosely call Doves. Another group might argue more hegemonically: we should accept the grim fact that humankind responds best and perhaps only to force, and therefore we must build the strength required to function as the world's policeman, helping our friends and countering our enemies wherever possible and at whatever cost. These we call Hawks.

There are obviously hundreds of positions between my version of the fable of the Doves and the Hawks, and there are even more extreme positions on either side. But stating the situation this way, I believe, makes one thing clear for our purposes: in *either* case, we will need a better-informed citizenry, more globally conversant professionals, and a world which knows more about us. It is therefore fair to assume that, whatever the American role in the world of the future is determined to be, we need a better means to internationalize our education systems, developing national sophistication about the rest of the world.

This to me is the central point: we must internationalize, we must do it well, and we must get on with it soon. The harder questions follow: How? Do *what*? For what purpose? What constitutes "better"? What is realistically achievable and what is not? Who does what? How is it financed? What comes first?

It is within neither my purposes nor my competence to analyze all the options these questions imply. It was Adlai Stevenson who reminded us that in public policy discussions the unearthing of profundities is much less important than the reiteration of the obvious. I believe it is obvious that Americans *must* know more about other cultures, whether their learning is formal or acquired by nonformal means like the media. It must also be obvious that other cultures need to know more about us, whether they learn it formally or nonformally, at home or in the United States. Finally, it must be obvious that these two aspects of international education are closely related.

For me, any definition of IE must include our nation's responsibility to teach others about us as well as ourselves about them. It is no easier to separate these two processes than it is to wash one hand. Indeed, our ignorance of the world may be far less dangerous than others' ignorance of us. Our attitudes toward foreign students here, our overseas USIA programs, the work abroad of our universities, our international programs and our foundations—all these must have high national priority in any approach to an interdependent world.

IE is not a field but rather an approach to all fields. The international approach in education must take place in every discipline. As interdependency affects and in turn is affected by every field and discipline and indeed by some not yet invented, so the understanding of interdependency influences all human knowledge. The international dimension cannot be excluded from study in any field: not every mathematician or computer scientist must be a cross-cultural polyglot but *some* must be, there should be enough of them to meet predictable needs, and they should exercise leadership in their respective fields on international issues.

Today it is still hard, despite impressive efforts, to acquire an M.B.A. with a strong dimension in international business and one or two fluent languages, at least for an American. Yet, in Louis Rukeyser's quip, our bounty lies over the ocean. It is as hard to get a law degree with an international component and language skills. Even IE graduates are not always proficient in foreign languages, perhaps because the State Department and other foreign affairs agencies still do not require in-depth proficiency in a language as a prerequisite for employment.

IE, and language and area studies, among other disciplines, have a special function: they train American professionals who will spend their lives in the work of foreign affairs, here and abroad. These practitioners require special attention quite different from that needed for the enlightened participating citizen.

International education, in other words, is an approach to learning that aims at two kinds of competence: professional expertise and citizen awareness. Each must take place both in the United States and with educated classes in other nations. Two kinds of competence, here and abroad: these are the four components of any definition of international education. These four elements lie at the heart of our nation's survival, in my judgment.

The responsibility for American citizen competence falls not only on American and foreign schools and universities, but on every element involved in the subtle business of nonformal education, most prominently the media. The second kind of competence, that of the professionals (including those in foreign affairs), is primarily a function of 200 or so graduate schools in America and some of their foreign counterparts. Each group presents a different challenge, but attention to one is pointless without parallel attention to the other. The education of foreign elites, abroad and in the United States, is handled by these same institutions and by extensions from them, through channels like the Fulbright program.

Both citizen and professional competence in international education have this in common: that the process of learning is as important as the product. How we learn, where we learn, how we discover what we do not know are as important as what we learn. The experience of living abroad matters as much as what we discover there—indeed, learning to live there is much of what we learn. In the professions, we need to know our disciplines. But we need to know how foreign professionals view the same knowledge, what they know that we do not, how they go about thinking through their work, making their decisions. We even need to know what they do *not* know, and what they reject of what *we* know, if we are to deal with them in the full understanding which validates exchange between us. By learning to see ourselves from outside our own culture, we escape the provincialism that makes interdependency a threat rather than a potential, a challenge or an attack rather than an opportunity, an enemy rather than a friend. We need to learn to read, not only books but ourselves and others. In Charles Frankel's words:

> *A primary purpose of educational and cultural exchange is to become aware of others' cultural codes and of our own, to bring to the surface the context of unspoken facts and assumptions within which their words and actions, and ours, can be correctly interpreted.*

With proper encouragement, Frankel's definition of reading could give new meaning to the three R's in American education and throughout the world.

Howard Perlmutter, the remarkable systems analyst and cross-cultural theorist of the Wharton School, has provided us with a simple yardstick by which we can judge progress along the path toward international sophistication. He notes that all negotiations, by which he means all human transactions up to the level of international relations, take place at four progressive levels.

At the first level, outright Warfare, there is no communication, and slogans rule. At the second level, we find the mode of Confrontation, in which two enemies or nonfriends, with minimal understanding or communication, try to agree, for example, on a cease-fire. Third comes a new kind of friendly association, which he calls Dialog: here both parties are friendly, there is much apparent communication, and the purpose is to reach an agreement which will be advantageous to both sides. Yet still the style is wary and defensive, as each partner, proud of his or her sovereignty, negotiaties to maximize his or her own interests.

The fourth level of negotiation he calls Design. This is the relationship that occurs in the best marriages and families, among teammates, or among interdependent survivors on a desert island. At the level of Design, the goal is to become something together that is greater that the sum of the single parts, to achieve something together that cannot be done alone.

Perlmutter notes that international relations, even in the best cases, seem permanently stalled at the level of Dialog. But he warns that day by day we are drawing nearer to an era when only Design relationships can assure global survival.

How does the United States get to the Design state, as a nation not entirely firm even in Dialog relationships with large parts of the world? The answer is not easy, if only because of the very historical and political impediments I have noted. Let us pretend to ourselves however that some realities *can* be changed, that some history *can* be overridden, that some things *can* become obvious in time, that the time *does* come for some ideas after all.

Beginning with professional competence, let us pretend we can see beyond the mountains: by the simple device of waving them away, perhaps we can think some presently unthinkable thoughts. Imagine, for example, a government so wise, an electorate so supportive, a leadership so awesome that a set of priorities and strategies *could* be devised and implemented. Let us assume that a vast national consensus exists on the need to become more internationally sophisticated in an interdependent world in peril. This is more than a pleasant fantasy: these magic-wand premises lead to some interesting guesses. Let me try to imagine with you some of the questions a Presidential Commission in such a land, appointed to deal with IE, might ask:

- Should we continue to allow funding and administrative support for international education to be parceled out to ten or fifteen different federal agencies, each with its own agenda and staff?

- Should first attention go to professional competence, with its relatively manageable target of graduate schools, or to citizen competence, with the vital agenda of changing national attitudes?

• Should we expect our top graduate schools to take the entire responsibility for funding all new dimensions in international learning when we have agreed it is a *national* priority?

• Should we still pretend to believe in the wishful concept of seeding then withdrawing from such funding?

• Should we expect the student-products of our universities to cover their own costs when we know that the harder the material the greater the cost (and perhaps the value)?

• Should such vital educational goals, within the university, be encapsulated in self-contained departments, or should we seek instead to open international dimensions in every graduate discipline, school, and profession?

• Do the market forces which govern our media rule out a deeper foreign affairs and cross-cultural dimension for our press and TV?

• Should rigid academic patterns like the four-year undergraduate curriculum impede the learning of hard language cultures, some of which require a lifetime of study? Should we place the burden of developing such vital national resources so predominantly on language teachers?

• Should we allow the products and programs of international education to go underevaluated and its process unresearched?

• Should the costly graduates of our educational investments be underutilized, underemployed, and unprotected, in their careers?

• In foreign affairs education, should we continue to vest all teaching and research in a nonpracticing priesthood, paying little more than lip service to the resource presented by experienced practitioners? Similarly, should the foreign affairs community avail itself so little of the international skills of our university experts?

• Should we allow the self-selecting, meaning only those who can afford it, to occupy the vast majority of foreign student desks in American universities?

• Should we continue to allow the 400,000 foreign elites on our shores to go undernourished? By like token, should we continue to ignore their potential for contributing to U.S. education?

• Should we allow the number and the qualifications of political appointments to the foreign affairs agencies to go unregulated? Should

our best people not be entitled to spend fully challenging careers in foreign affairs? Conversely, should we allow professionals to go forward in
their careers without periodic outside evaluation, without systematic
retraining, and without continued exposure to the products of research?

These questions, and so many others, spring to mind with a readiness that proves my point: *if* we could plan, *if* we had the power, the
questions are easy enough to frame and relatively easy to answer. *If*
we could plan, *if* we could free ourselves from past habits and turf-
linked agendas, could we not innovate focused and efficient
approaches to the training and skilling of professional personnel? And
if we could develop some way to focus our investment, i.e., the budg-
etary equivalent of planning, then would the actual investment
required to provide enough qualified professionals for the needs of
America in an interdependent world be *so* high? Would it cost as
much as a few training sorties by a squadron of F-18s?

You will recall I made all this easy by waving away reality. The
game is justified, I believe, by the perceptions it affords. Surely the
straightforward and obvious answers to the disingenuous questions
above imply that things can be done—one by one. Taken together, in
their interlocking relationship, they are harder. Together, they would
add up to a fair set of indicators, a kind of road map to show us the
way. Whether we then settle for half the distance or even less, some
simple indicative thinking along these lines would help us choose our
targets, set our sights, and move forward with least waste.

For professional competence, the funding picture will most certainly be bleak until we can find ways to focus our goals and thus our
investments. But even with focused goals, we have learned we cannot
count on federal funding alone: we must find alternative sources. Why
not explore the idea of greater investment by the end-users, e.g., the
employers, of international education's products? Why not encourage
more enlightened corporate support on grounds that the payoff over
time, and even in the shorter range (e.g. with regard to personnel
recruitment), will mean the survival or nonsurvival of those same corporations? Why not demand more cost sharing by the student, in the
form of long-term low-interest loans, perhaps in return for service to
the nation? And why not accept the simple central premise of almost
every nation in the world: that the national interest, when it pinpoints

a specific need, is best served by centralized (indicating planned) funding administered with sensitivity and wisdom?

For those who smell heresy in these questions, I remind you that heresy can only reside in an answer. Let me risk one, whatever the consequences. I believe that *focused* spending on professional competence, education, and research need not be so costly in comparative terms, especially if we can find ways to predict national needs, ensure better utilization, broaden the base of funding, and of course administer programs with wisdom and sensitivity.

Citizen competence, if only at minimal levels, is far more difficult. Here we are not dealing with a problem that can be solved with money, for we are talking of nothing less than revising national values. As Woodrow Wilson said of changing a curriculum, this is no more difficult than moving a cemetery. David Reisman once suggested, with regard to rethinking gender roles in the United States, that we could do a lot if a few more 270-pound football players taught kindergarten, art, and music and a few more ravishing, petite women taught chemistry, mathematics, physics, and metal-working shop. What is needed for this kind of change are the most priceless commodites of all, yet the cheapest: national will and towering leadership.

To internationalize our schools and our minds, we need do little more than convince ourselves as a nation that it matters to do so. When the public demands it, the universities and schools will respond. America has a unique ability to change, as demonstrated so convincingly in the last decades by the revolution in attitudes toward pollution and ecology.

When the heroes of our society—be they quarterbacks, (like "Twinkletoes" Fulbright), politicians, scientists, CEO's, front-line battle surgeons, generals, movie stars, automobile manufacturers, astronauts, the leads in *Dallas*, university presidents, or all of the above—when these heroes of our society routinely speak foreign languages with their overseas counterparts, when they consistently reveal impressive cross-cultural sensitivity and wisdom, when they invariably show a superb grasp of foreign affairs issues and world history, then this nation will follow closely behind. Remember: when a national survey revealed abysmal ignorance of the world by school children, they *did* know about Korea—thanks to Alan Alda.

How do we prepare to enter the era of Design? What values do we have to change to live with interdepencence? It boils down to a few big things and a few small. Above all we need to learn, for ourselves, and then to teach our children, to accept, cope with, manage, and understand change and its effects. Can we learn to treat change not as a threat but as our potential, our promise for tomorrow? Can we do this without adopting change for its own sake, without throwing out the good with the bad? Can we learn to manage change in the context of continuity?

Perhaps we need a few wise teachers, someone like practical old Ben Franklin. It is a diverting game to imagine Franklin at work today on a new edition of *Poor Richard's Almanac*. Collected from friends here and there, here are a few thoughts to be turned over to some maker of epigrams and aphorisms for tomorrow's world:

On Difference

Celebrate difference, do not fear it.

Difference is neither better nor worse, it is only different.

On Being Number One

Wanting to be Number One is the worst danger.

If winning is the *only* thing, what is everything else?

Nice guys may finish last, but after the game they are nicer.

Being Number One is the heaviest responsibility.

No one is Number One for long.

On Planning

Planning is hard work, and it tends to elitism, but when resources shrink there may be no alternative.

On Stereotyping

National stereotypes, like their racial brethren, are the crutches of crippled minds.

To generalize about national characteristics is to indulge in a subtle form of racism.

On Identity and Sovereignty

Finding and projecting an identity matters as much for societies, cultures, nations, and perhaps even globes as it does for individuals.

Nothing is more irreducible than personal and national sovereignty, with the possible exception of human folly.

On Language Learning

A language learned is a furrow upturned.

On Friends and Neighbors

Treasure an ally, there is no asset more rare.

Respecting and admiring your neighbor may matter more than loving him.

On Problem Solving

Problems increase geometrically, solutions mathematically (the Issawi-Wilcox Principle).

And my favorite, borrowed from Robert Beckman:

On IE

For the Founding Fathers, ''international education'' was a redundancy.

Education is more than mottoes and slogans, and the real work will have to be done within the classrooms and in those mysterious rooms where curricular changes are mulled and textbooks written. Is it truly asking too much that this nation, led by its great men and women, reexamine its basic values and find ways of reflecting them in every communication mode that can shape a mind? Is it too much to ask English teachers to present English as only one language of many, marvelously gifted at some things and less so at others, and owing its very existence to the generous loans and cooperation of dozens of other languages?

Is it too much for them to remind their students from the start that some people live their entire lives without speaking English and are no less for that? Could not mathematics teachers remind their students, from virtually the first day of class, that numbers and mathematical thought have a history, that mathematics is a cumulative wisdom reflecting contributions from all over the world and from all periods of history, and even from the Arabs (to indulge in a counter-stereotype)? Is it too hard for music teachers to present the Western diatonic-tempered scale as a simplifying convention adopted by a relatively small segment of the world's musicians?

Is it too hard for historians to develop comparative techniques? For science to be taught historically? For business schools to use foreign and international case studies, perhaps even in the original languages? For churches to accept it as part of their role to shed light on the virtues of other religions as well as their own? Is it so difficult to teach our children, and ourselves, that America is only one patch of our bright blue globe?

AFTERWORD

I began by asking what, in this our beloved United States in the year 1984, we mean by international education. I hope we have concluded, together, that it is our means to survival. We have come a long way, midst the confusion of the scholar's questions, the bureaucrat's assertions, and the teacher's dramatizations. If you have been able to distinguish one from the other, then I have failed. On the other hand, if I leave in your minds the simple formula that IE equals survival, then perhaps it has been worthwhile.

It is tempting to forgo the wise tradition of the public lecture and *not* end with a joke. One story, however, has special meaning for me, and I beg your indulgence for a final moment of sharing. Thirty-five years ago, my country invested in me and I left the United States to journey to France as a Fulbright fellow. In mid-October of 1949, on the eve of our departure, 200 of us were sent off with a modest reception in the handsome offices of the French cultural attaché in New York.

This wise, distinguished, and farsighted gentleman related to us the fable of the anthill and the golfer. When the golf ball first landed on the anthill, the ants were unconcerned. But after the hapless golfer had made two unsuccessful chops at it, reducing the ant population by some 50 percent, the ants assembled in committee, in the way of ants. After much deliberation, during which a third chop dispatched another segment of the population, the ants passed a resolution. It read like this: "If we want to survive, we'd better get on the ball."

Thirty-five years ago, that story was elegant and amusing. Today, alas, it is grim.

BIBLIOGRAPHY

The following list of key publications on aspects of cultural diplomacy may serve better the purposes of this article.

Philip H. Coombs, *The Fourth Dimension of Foreign Policy* (New York: Harper and Row, 1964).

J. Manuel Espinosa, *Inter-American Beginnings of U.S. Cultural Diplomacy, 1938–1948* Washington: USGPO).

Wilma Fairbank, *America's Cultural Experiment in China, 1942–1949* (Washington: USGPO, 1976).

Charles Frankel, *High on Foggy Bottom: An Outsider's Inside View of the Government* (New York: Harper and Row, 1969), p. 240.

Charles Frankel, *The Neglected Aspect of Foreign Affairs* (Washington: Brookings Institution, 1966).

Walter Johnson and Francis J. Colligan, *The Fulbright Program: A History* (Chicago: University of Chicago Press, 1965).

Henry I. Kellerman, *Cultural Relations as an Instrument of Foreign Policy: The Educational Exchange Program Between the United States and Germany, 1945–1954* (Washington: USGPO, 1978).

Frank A. Nincovich, *The Diplomacy of Ideas: U.S. Foreign Policy and Cultural Relations, 1938–1950* (Cambridge, Mass.: Cambridge University Press, 1981).

Lois W. Roth, ''Public Diplomacy and the Past: The Search for an American Style of Propaganda, 1952–1977,'' *The Fletcher Forum, VIII, 2* (Summer 1984), pp. 353–396.

Laurence A. Wylie and Sarella Henriquez, ''French Images of American Life,'' *Tocqueville Review, IV, 2* (Fall–Winter 1982), pp. 176–274.

TWO

The Third Goal: Uncovering America's Hidden Heart

Loret M. Ruppe

Loret Miller Ruppe has been the director of the Peace Corps since 1981. Prior to her appointment, Mrs. Ruppe was an active volunteer and volunteer organizer for a variety of efforts. She served as chair of the Houghton, Michigan, United Fund Campaign, as president of the St. Joseph's Hospital Guild, and as president of the International Neighbor Club IV in Washington, D.C. In addition to being a volunteer with charity and civic organizations, she has also been an active political volunteer, working with the Houghton County Republican Committee and in the congressional campaigns of her husband, Philip Ruppe, who served as a representative from 1966 to 1979. In 1980, she served as co-chair of Michigan's Reagan/Bush State Committee.

President Reagan, in declaring 1983 as the National Year of Voluntarism, summed up much of the Peace Corps experience when he said, "Voluntarism is a cornerstone of the American way of life and a fundamental characteristic of our American heritage." Today, the Peace Corps, now into its third decade, has become a part of that "American heritage" to which the President referred. That is why I am particularly happy to discuss the Peace Corps with you, and specifically what we call the third goal: what has come back to America—what nearly 100,000 returned volunteers over many years have done to enrich American society and the pursuit of international education through sharing the understanding gained by their Peace Corps experience of peoples and cultures around the world.

Twenty-three years ago a tired presidential candidate found himself in front of a crowd of cheering students and townspeople. That candidate was John F. Kennedy at the University of Michigan campus.

It was the last campaign stop of a long and exhausting night at two o'clock in the morning. The date: October 10, 1960. The weather, fortunately, was mild, but those 10,000 people who crowded the steps of the student union would have been there no matter what the weather. Moved by the enthusiasm of the crowd, Kennedy tossed out a challenge—to spend years in "Africa or Latin America or Asia working for the United States and working for freedom." He appealed to the willingness of those young people to "contribute part of your life to this country." And thus, in that early morning in 1960, the Peace Corps idea—giving life and form to idealism—grew into flame.

Now, on a college campus twenty-three years later, I want to tell you about how that great vision has grown and matured, yet how it must always remain bright because the vision is so right, so in harmony with human nature, so correct in an age of global interdependence. I want to tell you how I feel about it, how I know that it has lived up and is still living up to the dreams and hopes and pragmatic beliefs of its earliest supporters.

Its founders and its creators, and there were many, settled on three goals for this new vision of the Peace Corps, but they were three goals with one overriding purpose: the promotion of world peace and friendship. What were these three goals? They were defined by the United States Congress in 1961:

- To help the people of interested countries and areas in meeting their needs for trained manpower;

- To create a better understanding of Americans on the part of the peoples served; and

- To help promote a better understanding of other peoples on the part of Americans.

These goals are as important today as they were over twenty years ago, and they are as valid in the 1980s as they were in the 1960s, still consistent with the needs and dreams of both the developing world and our own country.

How, then, has this organization, this Peace Corps—a government program paid for by your tax dollars, staffed by dedicated Americans—how has the Peace Corps fulfilled these three goals?

From the beginning, the Peace Corps has paid a great deal of attention to its *first* goal—providing technical assistance to the less-developed countries of the world. In my testimony to Congress earlier in 1983, I noted examples of current productive Peace Corps activities concerning that first goal of meeting the development needs of Third World countries:

• 1500 volunteers provided technical assistance in agricultural and rural development projects and taught fisheries development which provided a source of food protein as well as income to rural communities.

• 165 renewable energy and appropriate technology volunteers worked on energy-conserving stoves, charcoal production, solar food drying, and biogas production. Another 475 volunteers worked in the same areas in secondary projects.

• 200 volunteers served as planners and supervisors of the construction of small dams, spillways, and irrigation canals in rural areas, also providing assistance with potable water systems.

• 1000 volunteers worked on health education and community health organization; and 200 volunteers assisted in developing village sanitation systems.

These are but several notable examples of meeting this first goal of the Peace Corps.

Objective evaluation studies over the years have provided ample evidence of effectiveness in achieving this first goal. In a research project in the 1960s, Cornell University studied fifty Peace Corps volunteers and their impact on villages in the Peruvian Andes. A major finding was that Peace Corps communities developed at a rate almost three times as fast as those without volunteers. That finding is not uncommon. On a larger scale, it was also pointed out that during one single month prior to this survey, Peace Corps volunteers had a direct impact on the lives of nearly one million people. In this sense, the Peace Corps' greatest impact has always been at the individual or local level. One of my predecessors, former Director Jack Vaughn, once said, "The economists ask us, 'Does it really make a difference what a handful of Peace Corps volunteers accomplished in a small, forgotten village of the Andes?' " To Vaughn, as to most volunteers, the answer was obvious: "Yes," he said, "it makes a difference to that village." There are, quite literally, tens of thousands of stories of Peace Corps Volunteers making a difference to individual lives in towns and villages around the world.

This kind of micro-level impact should not be underestimated. In the 1970s, development experts recognized that in too many cases massive transfers of capital to the governments of the Third World countries has failed to "trickle down" and improve the condition of people at the lowest socioeconomic levels, particularly the people of the rural areas. A grassroots approach, aimed at directly meeting the basic human needs of the poor, was proposed as an alternative. The Peace Corps, it soon became apparent, had long been a forerunner of this approach. So, ironically enough, in meeting its first goal, the Peace Corps organization was—and I am proud to say still is—an extremely important model for "new" approaches to development.

How have we dealt with the *second* goal of the Peace Corps—to develop a better understanding of Americans among foreign peoples in whose countries the Peace Corps serves? There is no doubt that Peace Corps volunteers, with their dedication and unique enthusiasm, have shown the outside world a different kind of American from the one normally on view.

This I can validate from my own experience. In the nearly three years I have been Director of the Peace Corps, I have traveled to thirty-one of the sixty-one countries where there is a Peace Corps presence. Why do I travel? Because from the beginning, I knew that we were and and are here in Washington to support those dedicated 5000 volunteers overseas. For it is they who deserve the best we can give—the best we can give in recruitment, training, placement, and programming. They deserve the best because they are an extension to the developing world of what is best in America: commitment, caring, sharing, and that spirit of voluntarism which President Reagan has encouraged.

So I travel to avoid the Washington "ivory tower" syndrome. I travel to see firsthand, to talk with the leaders of the countries in which our volunteers serve. I travel to visit American staff, our Country Directors, and trainers in each country, to talk with the four-fifths of our total staff overseas who are "Host Country Nationals," citizens of the countries where the Peace Corps serves. It is these foreign nationals, really the unsung heroes of the Peace Corps, who furnish, in many cases, the continuity, sensitivity, and special insights that make the Peace Corps worthy of the credibility it has around the world.

However, I travel most of all to visit the volunteers, to find out from them firsthand how they are doing, to answer their questions, and to find out what we can perhaps do better to support their efforts from Washington. It is an unending dialogue and one most essential for the fulfillment of the mission of the Peace Corps.

My 1983 trip took me to West Africa. I spoke with President Siaka Stevens of Sierra Leone, a country where the Peace Corps has worked for over twenty years. President Stevens said to me, "Peace Corps volunteers have served as a bridge between the people of Sierra Leone and the people of the United States . . . . It is the people-to-people relationships that cement friendships between nations." In Upper Volta in November 1983, President Sankara, after reading the letter I had brought with me from President Reagan, noted, "It is important for President Reagan and me, as President of Upper Volta, to be friends, but it is far more important that there be friendship between the people of the United States and the people of Upper Volta."

But in accomplishing these links, the Peace Corps experience is often a veritable baptism by fire. A former volunteer in Ethiopia referred to it as "a collision of different values and different expectations, of values that are never wholly transferable, of expectations that are never fully realized." And there we confront the cultural challenge of what may well be the real meaning of the Peace Corps: as one volunteer phrased it, "the call to go, not where man has never been before, but where he has lived differently; the call to experience firsthand the intricacies of a different culture, to understand from the inside rather than the outside, and to test the limits of one's own way of life against another."

How can we describe this cultural awakening? I can think of no better example than that of the volunteer (still, by the way, working for the Peace Corps here in Washington) who worked in a small town in Costa Rica. He had initiated road-digging, bridge-building, and a water system. However, he saw his real challenge in getting local religious groups to work together. It was an uphill battle. Yet at his farewell party he recalled his insight this way: "We had broken through the culture, the religion, to see each other as people."

"To see each other as people"—that is an appropriate theme for the Peace Corps of the 1980s. Or as the volunteer who came back from Zaire told his former hosts, "Your children are mine. I feel your words and see your heart." But this was, and still most certainly is, a two-way process. Through the efforts of 100,000 volunteers, the peoples of developing countries have felt the words and seen the hidden heart of America.

This hidden heart of America leads us to the *third* goal of the Peace Corps—the impact on American society of these 100,000 returned Peace Corps volunteers. But to really see how this "fundamental characteristic of our American heritage," as President Reagan called voluntarism, came about, let us briefly glance back some half a century, and look at our country as it was then.

Woodrow Wilson was President when the American people rejected an international leadership role for the United States. He confronted the classic American tradition of isolationism and parochialism and was at the forefront of a historic trend toward a more active world role for the United States. He was right in his larger vision as were other Presidents who followed, and it is the Peace Corps which has, half a century later, helped validate Wilson's dream of an American internationalism dedicated to a major American role in the interdependent world of today.

The Peace Corps is, indeed, a remarkable concept. Never in the history of the world, in peacetime, has any nation sent forth to foreign lands so many of its citizens to work and live among the inhabitants of those countries, and then brought them back to their own nation. Today, from New York to Florida, from Alaska to California, more than 100,000 former Peace Corps volunteers have resumed their American lives, forever changed by their Peace Corps experience. They do all kinds of things, occupy all kinds of positions in government, other international development agencies, academia, and private industry.

Three years ago, in my first major address as director of the Peace Corps, I said that we as a nation must better recognize the experience of Peace Corps volunteers who have worked at the grass roots with the people of other nations. Having participated in what undoubtedly is one of the world's most unique graduate studies programs, these Peace Corps volunteers represent one of the most valuable resources which this country has, a resource that deserves to be better appreciated, developed, and tapped.

I still firmly believe that, and I am not alone in my belief. The recent report of the Commission on Security and Economic Assistance (the Carlucci Commission) established by the President to encourage public support of foreign assistance, noted that "The growing ranks of more than 100,000 returned Peace Corps volunteers have a significant impact on Americans' awareness of the developing world." The report also noted that returned Peace Corps volunteers have an active network and an ongoing interest in international affairs and suggested that such a group "could provide the nucleus around which a broader-based information system could form" which could help educated an unfortunately parochial American public to the realities of America's role in global relations today.

The Commission report noted the necessity for our foreign assistance programs to recognize the great diversity and changing needs of developing nations. It recommended the promotion of a "citizens' network" of Americans who have a direct interest in programs of foreign assistance. Returned Peace Corps volunteers would play a valuable role in such a citizens' network. The report specifically called on the Administration and Congress to continue support for development education, a theme directly relevant to the Peace Corps' third goal concerns, for who better to educate the American people about the development issues of the Third World than those who have worked and lived in those countries?

That, in part, is what was meant by the third goal of the Peace Corps. As President Kennedy said in a special message to the Congress of the United States on March 1, 1961, returned Peace Corps volunteers "will return better able to assume the responsibilities of American citizenship and with a greater understanding of our global responsibilities."

The first director of the Peace Corps, Sargent Shriver, in a speech delivered before the Los Angeles World Affairs Council in October, 1965, said that

Probably the most important development in the future of the Peace Corps will be the impact of returning volunteers on American society. Before long, 5000 Peace Corps volunteers a year will be returning from having lived and worked overseas, under difficult conditions, among strange cultures, lands, and people. They will be a new breed of Americans, or rather the revival of an old breed of Americans—the Americans who believed everything was possible to the man of determination, the Americans who believed some things were more important than material affluence or personal success.

Shriver spoke in terms of the future of this "new breed of Americans," the returned Peace Corps volunteers. They are among us now, and that future that Shriver spoke of is today. That third goal, as quoted in the Peace Corps Act—"A better understanding of other peoples on the part of the American people"—is now being realized throughout the United States, in Congress and statehouses, in international development agencies and other branches of our federal government, on campuses, in private industry, in small towns and suburban enclaves throughout this nation.

Our concerns for the Peace Corps' third goal are not just American concepts: Indian Prime Minister Nehru once said, "In matters of the spirit, I am sure young Americans would learn a good deal in this country and it could be an important experience for them." Nehru sensed that an Indian villager's need to acquire certain technical skills to build a dam or a school was matched by the need of the people of the United States to acquire a deeper insight into the ways of the Third World.

The renowned social scientist David Riesman predicted that the greatest impact of the Peace Corps might well be in the United States when volunteers returned. And it is true, I firmly believe, that with the peace of the world resting to a great extent on the ability of Americans—*all* Americans—to deal with the realities of global interdependence, the 100,000 returned volunteers must be even stronger spokespersons for the need to develop shared perceptions of, and solutions to, world problems in the 1980s and beyond. Reflecting this concern, a 1969 Harris poll noted that the majority of returned volunteers saw the United States' major international problem as that of adapting its foreign policy to meet the needs of the Third World. Lending impact to this perception, eight years later a study showed that most former volunteers felt America's greatest problem was the failure to respect the value systems of other countries.

Other studies have shown, however, that most former volunteers resume lives that, in many ways, resemble those of the majority of other Americans. They return to school, begin careers, marry, and start families. Nevertheless, there is enough evidence to suggest that beneath the surface of this picture of normality, there is something "exceptional" about returned volunteers and their impact upon American society.

How can we quantify this impact? Is it possible, or even desirable, to put numbers on such an experience? In another Louis Harris poll of former volunteers, 81 percent of them said they felt very different from others of their ages and backround for having had the Peace Corps experience. There is no doubt, then, that these 100,000 Americans have undergone a dramatic change. As one returned volunteer put it, "Whatever we were before, and none of us can quite remember, that's all gone."

Studies conducted so far have shown, however, that this Peace Corps experience does not radically alter volunteers' career preferences. Rather, it catalzyes their interests and propels the returnees down the road they would probably have taken only after a much longer period of decision making. Which roads have returned volunteers taken? Roughly 15 percent of returnees have taken up positions with government organizations at home and overseas (the national average is 3 percent), thus realizing the initial hope of the founders of the Peace Corps that the Peace Corps would provide a steady flow of experienced personnel to the Foreign Service, the Agency for International Development, the State Department and so forth.

In late 1983, I recieved a letter from the United States Ambassador to Indonesia. He attached a list of former Peace Corps volunteers who are now assigned to the United States Embassy in Jakarta, together with their years and countries of service. The twenty-five ranged in years of service from 1963 to 1980, in countries such as Upper Volta, Nigeria, Liberia, Guatemala, Indoneisa, the Philippines, Iran, Sierra Leone, India, Turkey, Malaysia, Afghanistan, Ethiopia, and Malawi. The Ambassador closed the letter by saying that he looked forward to welcoming even larger numbers of former volunteers to serve at his post.

In Cameroon, in 1981, more than 40 percent of AID personnel had been volunteers, and every one of the fifty-five AID missions around the world has at least one former volunteer on its staff. Nearly 40 percent of the employees of CARE are former volunteers. The Experiment in International Living estimated that at least half its staff was comprised of returned volunteers. The list of private voluntary organizations where returned volunteers play major roles has barely begun with these citations.

The private business sector has also been a beneficiary of the skills and experience of returned Peace Corps volunteers. Many international companies and banks have made a point of hiring former volunteers. As Fulton Boyd, director of corporate development for the Brazilian subsidiary of Adela (a multinational investment company), explained it: "Former Peace Corps members have the languages, they're well integrated into the community, they know how to travel and they adapt very well to dollars and cents." During a recent trip I made to the Chase Manhattan Bank, seven out of ten officers in that institution's African division were former Peace Corps Volunteers. Over twenty former volunteers serve in management positions at Chase.

But perhaps the most exciting and profound impact of returned volunteers has been in the field of education. In the 1960s, 26 percent of returnees went into schoolteaching at home. In the 1970s, 27 percent were employed by various educational institutions. Nearly 60 percent of all former volunteers have attempted to further their own education in one way or another. In 1980, the Peace Corps polled universities in an attempt to evaluate just what effects returned volunteers have had on teaching methods, curriculum development and academic standards in general. Not surprisingly, the response was overwhelmingly favorable. Former Peace Corps volunteers bring an international dimension to their studies and to their contacts with their colleagues.

This international dimension has been epitomized, to take one specific example, by the returnees' knowledge of foreign languages. For over two decades, the Peace Corps has given instruction in hundreds of different languages and dialects, a significant number of which had never been taught before in the United States. Indeed, at a time when fewer and fewer Americans are learning a foreign language, the Peace Corps has become one of the nation's most innovative language-learning institutions.

The foreign language contributions of the Peace Corps to our nation become even more apparent in the light of conclusions of the recent study by the National Commission on Excellence in Education:

- No states require high school students to study foreign languages;

- Only 13 percent of all high school students in the nation complete one year of French;

- Only 16 percent of all high school students in the nation complete one year of geography;

- Finally, only one-fifth of America's colleges and universities have foreign langauge requirements for admission, and the Commission reports a severe shortage of foreign language instructors in the United States.

But what have been the benefits to American society of the volunteers' sharing of their experience, not only in government and education, but also in the myriad of communities where they have returned to live and become opinion-leaders? I would submit that one of the major benefits of these experiences has been to take some of the fear and mystery out of the American view of the Third World. Only twenty years ago, many Americans considered it a dangerous prospect to send young people into what was still referred to as "darkest Africa." The psychological impact and educational value of innumerable stories and photographs of Peace Corps volunteers feeding and teaching African, Asian and Latin American children should not be underestimated. On returning home, volunteers have often tried to reinforce this awareness through private conversations, public discussion, and action.

But so much more needs to be done. We have only to look at the growing return to isolationist feeling here in America, as evidenced by the lack of public support for foreign assistance to which the Carlucci Commission referred.

One of the most successful channels for public awareness actions has been the Peace Corps Partnership Program. Begun in 1964, this highly successful program encourages people in host countries to plan and complete their own self-help projects with the support of American sponsors. Returned volunteers have often been the originators of partnership ideas. These projects have varied from the construction of

classrooms or cisterns to the purchase of oxen for an agricultural training program. Since the Partnership Program's inception, over 3000
self-help community projects have been inititaed in various developing countries.

The Peace Corps Partnerships have often had a remarkable effect
in expanding the horizons of Americans. I am reminded of a small
community in the Ozarks. The motto of the local newspaper is
"Shannon County First—the World Afterward." People in this community tell the story of the little girl who told her local clergyman
about her new teacher, a "foreigner." "Where is she from?" asked
the reverend. "St. Louis," the little girl replied. Today, thanks to the
efforts of former Peace Corps volunteers and the agency's Partnership
Program, Shannon County is now the proud sponsor of a palm oil
project in Borkeza, a small community located about 225 miles north-
east of Liberia's capital city, Monrovia. It may still be "Shannon
County First—the World Afterward," but the world has developed a
little through this partnership, and so has Shannon County.

But how to organize these volunteers, how to channel their experiences into something more? That was the question and, to a large
degree, still is. One response in 1978 was to establish, for the first
time, a National Council of Returned Peace Corps Volunteers. Its
purpose was to organize a network of local returned volunteer groups
all across the country and encourage former volunteers to share their
perceptions and experiences. What we have found through these
organizations is that returned volunteers do not want to relive the
Peace Corps experience in the way that college alumni fantasize about
long ago campus events. On the contrary, service as a Peace Corps
volunteer typically seems to have been so profound an experience that
it cannot later be evoked without some pain and reluctance.

This is, indeed, a new kind of American, this returned Peace Corps
volunteer. No former volunteer is neutral about his or her experience,
or indifferent to the fate of the organization which made it possible,
and it is this *lack* of neutrality that has made the returned Peace Corps
volunteer such an articulate and fervent spokesperson for a greater
understanding of the Third World on the part of the people of the
United States.

This effort to bring the world home to Americans has resulted in
what appeared on my desk in 1983: an articulate and well-researched

proposal from the National Council of Returned Peace Corps Volunteers, whose headquarters is in Nebraska, for the creation of a Development Education Program.

The proposal notes the "special senstitivity, insight and commitment of Third World development" on the part of returned volunteers, and emphasizes that these qualities should not be lost to American society. The Development Education Program, as outlined, will assist former volunteers to integrate their overseas experience in the American context through a process of sharing their knowledge in their own communities. The Development Education Program as submitted would pursue four main objectives:

1. Reinforcing the concept of development education to Peace Corps volunteers during service and training;
2. Providing technical assistance for returned Peace Corps volunteers in development education;
3. Offering a series of regional training workshops with local world hunger organizations and private voluntary organizations and;
4. Targeting new populations of returned volunteers for support and participation in development education.

This proposal will receive my serious consideration and full-hearted support.

Development education, as the Carlucci Commission report noted, is now an urgent need. In late 1983, a report was prepared entitled "A Framework for Development Education in the United States." The study, done by representatives of several private voluntary organizations, notes the significant "impact of global interdependence on both our own and the Third World peoples' daily lives." It emphasizes that development education has the responsibility of bringing about behavorial change as it addresses the critical problems and unique opportunities of our global society.

Development education, then, has perhaps achieved an unsurpassed measure of acceptance by those involved with it—the Carlucci Commission, this joint working group of private voluntary organizations, and the National Council of Returned Peace Corps Volunteers. We will continue to seek opportunities through increased collaboration with these and other groups, including USAID, so that the

unique experiences of former Peace Corps volunteers can be best utilized in this most important undertaking.

I am not the only one who values this Peace Corps experience;
today, thirty-five schools have reserved scholarships or graduate
assistantships for returned volunteers. Twelve schools, among them
The American University, the University of Connecticut, Michigan
State and Rutgers, grant academic credit, even toward master's
degrees, based on Peace Corps experience or training. We continually
seek to encourage more such recognition, and want to note the possi-
bility of universities' extending such credit toward graduate work
done overseas during the volunteers' service. In this area, and in others, the Peace Corps staff continues to work with a number of universities to try to improve and develop projects of common interest,
including the design of academic experiences of returned Peace Corps
volunteers.

But where are they all, these 100,000? And what has been their
impact on American Society? As a colleague said, "I can't prove anything, but I can only imagine that their impact has been significant."

And, in the end, we can prove nothing, or only a little, if empirical
proof is what we seek. But when it comes to changed attitudes, altered
perceptions, and a deeper perception of the rest of the world, these are
elements that do not lend themselves easily to statistics, or cold numbers. Even if we total up all the volunteers in all the returned members' groups, we reach perhaps several thousand. But where are all
the rest? To solve this riddle is as difficult as throwing a stone into a
lake and watching the ripples spread. You know that their effect
reaches all the way to the opposite shore, but you can't *see* all the way
across to that new shore. Yet somehow you still believe. For it is a law
of nature. One could stretch the metaphor and picture 100,000 stones
thrown into an ocean, each one picking up in effect where its predecessor left off. Those "ripples" would spread across an ocean—or, to
be more precise, across the geography of this entire country.

I have another idea, one which perhaps philosophically sums up all
I have said before. I continue to believe that the returned Peace Corps
volunteers are special and unique, for they know something that most
Americans do not know or have never learned.

What they have learned is that the meeting of idealism and reality,
of principle and pragmatism, need not always result in an uneasy

compromise, but rather in a more precise and exact perception of this country and the world. The strength of the returned Peace Corps volunteers resides in the best traditions of our own society. In a country where, throughout our history, there has been an uneasy relationship between principle and pragmatism, the returned Peace Corps volunteers, perhaps better than any other individuals of our society, blend the two in a superior fashion. In them, subsequent to their two years overseas, reality meets the ideal, pragmatism encounters principle. The United States has been a country of ideals, ever since its founding; yet it is a country that has, at the same time, prided itself upon its pragmatism, the "can-do" attitude of which we are all justly proud.

The Peace Corps volunteers have lived with both. The ideals which motivate them to join the Peace Corps and serve their country, or even serve themselves, meet the harsh light of reality in a mountain village in Ecuador or the jungles of Zaire or the sands of Tunisia. And somehow the volunteers come through it all, tempered by a passage through fire, as it were, and coming out stronger on the other side. I would submit to you today that no experience available to any American other than the Peace Corps can do that, and produce the kind of American that results from that experience. And to think there are 100,000 of them among us today, all of them, whether we realize it or not, throwing stones into their respective lakes and creating their own special kinds of ripple effects.

This is, of course, not a new notion, this direct relationship between what happens here in the United States and across the world. Theodore Roosevelt, in an address to the Nobel Prize Committee in 1907, sensed it when he said, "In our modern civilization it is as essential to secure a righteous peace based upon sympathy and fair dealing between the different classes of society as it is to secure such a peace among the nations of the earth." "A righteous peace," he called it, reflecting what America has always stood for, both here and abroad, and what former volunteers seek today. President Reagan spoke of it also, this time in 1980, when he called for a restoration, in our time, "of the American spirit of voluntary service, of cooperation, of private and community initiative; a spirit that flows like a deep and mighty river through the history of our nation." That "spirit of volunteer service" to which the President referred remains alive and well among the 5000 volunteers now serving overseas. It remains alive and well, to the benefit of all Americans, among those 100,000 to whom we continue to look to provide us with a picture of reality which is, perhaps, beyond our own perceptions.

What can we say, finally, about the impact on our society of these 100,000 pragmatic idealists? It has been said that a person gazing on the stars is at the mercy of the puddles on the road. While it is in the nature of humankind to want to leave some monument, however small, however insignificant, however intangible, to those who follow, we are no Don Quixotes tilting madly at windmills, no "Men of La Mancha" creating illusions. And we do not dream impossible dreams, but rather those which lead to the reality of world peace.

The Peace Corps is an answer to what the rest of the world needs most, as well as an answer to what Americans need most. It remains true to that "American way of life" that the President referred to and continues to shine as a beacon so "characteristic of our American heritage."

This heritage is now a reality, demonstrated by the Peace Corps volunteers who have finally come home, 100,000 strong, in what is a unique movement in the history both of our country and of the world. May their numbers continue to increase, bringing the world back home to America and making us all better because of it.

The Peace Corps has compiled a list of global organizations that have collected or produced materials on development education. It includes curricula, films, and resource directories. A copy of this list may be obtained from Dean William C. Olson, School of International Service, The American University, 4400 Massachusetts Avenue, N.W., Washington, D.C. 20016.

THREE

Toward Understanding Central America and United States Policy: The Role of the Press

Karen DeYoung

Karen DeYoung has been foreign editor of the Washington Post *since 1981. After receiving her degree in Journalism and Communications from the University of Florida in 1971, she served as a freelance reporter in South Central and Southeast Asia. After a period as a feature writer with the St. Petersburg, Florida* Times, *she worked as a freelance reporter in Western Africa. She came to the* Washington Post *in 1975 and, after a period on the Metropolitan staff, became the* Post's *Latin America correspondent, reporting from there during the period of the Nicaraguan revolution. She continued her coverage of Latin America after becoming deputy foreign editor in 1979. She was the 1980 winner of the Sigma Delta Chi Award for foreign reporting and the 1981 Marie Moors Cabot Award for promoting inter-American understanding.*

"Public opinion wins wars," Supreme Allied Commander General Dwight D. Eisenhower told a meeting of American newspaper editors in the spring of 1944. News media correspondents were the principal informers of public opinion, and as far as Eisenhower was concerned, the correspondents covering World War II were a valuable part of the war effort. Correspondents accredited to his headquarters, Eisenhower told the editors, were considered "quasi–staff officers."

During the invasion at Normandy, Eisenhower took four correspondents along to his advanced headquarters, and gave them long special briefings as the allies pushed inland. Although the element of surprise was crucial for the invasion to succeed, the allies deemed informing the public worth the possible security risk of accrediting a total of 538 journalists and photographers to cover the D-Day landing itself. According to later accounts of the press coverage, the correspondents sent 700,000 words back home on the first day of the invasion.

Nearly forty years later, a comparatively small contigent of American soldiers landed on a tiny island in the Caribbean and seized control in a surprise military operation. Not only were no correspondents accredited to accompany the invasion of Grenada, the Pentagon had made a specific decision prior to the beginning of the operation to permit no press to cover the events of October 1983, until the island itself had been secured and the operation was virtually over.

A small group of correspondents who had correctly anticipated the invasion and made it to Grenada themselves were effectively prohibited from filing their stories for two days, first by a lack of outside communications facilities and later by the United States military. The United States admiral in charge of the invasion said, perhaps in jest, that any American reporters who attempted to reach the island independently by air or sea could expect to be fired upon by American forces.

It was not until more than forty-eight hours after the invasion began that a small contingent of reporters, transported by the United States military and restricted to a radius of a few hundred yards, arrived on Grenada and provided the first independent coverage of the operation.

The American press was outraged at its exclusion from an event of such great concern to the American people. At least initially, the American government tried to placate the media. Administration spokespeople talked of problems of secrecy and security and safety— both for the troops and for the reporters—that had led to the decision to make the invasion off limits for the press. But later, in public comments and private conversations, another reason seemed to take precedence. The government simply did not trust the press to tell the right story.

World War II was different. Secretary of State George Shultz said.

Reporters were taken along with the troops because, on the whole, the reporters were "on our side."

At a December 1983, news conference, President Reagan expanded on Shultz's remarks. "Sometimes," the President said, "beginning with the Korean conflict and certainly in the Vietnam conflict, there was more criticizing of our own forces and what we were trying to do, to the point that it didn't seem that there was much criticism being leveled at the enemy. And sometimes, I just wish that we could get together on what is of importance to our national security in a situation of that kind, what is endangering our forces, and what is helping them in their mission."

For many Americans, particularly those of the generation that lived through World War II and the Korean War, press criticism and skepticism of United States forces in combat was something that began with Vietnam, the war that many in this country believe was lost by the media. But the battle between the media and government over what the public should know, who should control information in a conflict, and "whose side" the press should be on began long before Vietnam. In fact, World War II and the Korean War, where censorship reigned and correspondents willingly joined as part of their country's war effort, emerge as aberrations in a long, historical struggle in this country and in much of the West, in which Grenada may turn out to be only a minor footnote.

William Howard Russell's accounts to the *Times of London* in 1854 of British losses during the Charge of the Light Brigade sent shock waves through an English public that had been led by official military accounts to believe its forces were scoring overwhelming victories against the Russians in the Crimean War.

Before Russell's dispatches, most British newspapers took their reports from junior military offices assigned by their commanders to cover the war. But through the reports of Russell and others, Britons learned of the poor state of readiness of their soldiers, the inefficient command structure and the lack of medical supplies. As public support for the war began to wane and protests rose, the British government began its own media counterattack, censoring independent reports from the front, pressuring those newspapers whose correspondents had filed the offending stories, and sending its own reporters and photographers to the front to record happy, well-fed, and well-clothed soldiers.

A few years later, the American military had its first confrontation with the press during the U.S. Civil War. While the Confederate leadership imposed strict censorship of reports from the front, the Union forces struggled with the burdens of a free press.

In early 1863, *New York Herald* reporter Thomas W. Knox evaded censorship imposed by General William T. Sherman on coverage of battles at Vicksburg and Chickasaw and, along with other Northern correspondents, reported heavy casualties. Enraged, Sherman ordered Knox arrested and court-martialed as a spy. General Sherman wrote to a fellow officer: "The spirit of anarchy seems deep at work at the North, more alarming than the battalions that shell us from the opposite shore. Reporters print their limited and tainted observations as the history of events they neither see nor comprehend."

Knox was convicted and sentenced to banishment from the western front commanded by Sherman. When Sherman heard that President Lincoln had agreed to intervene in the case, he wrote to his wife: "I will never again command an army in America, if we must carry along paid spies . . . I will banish myself to some foreign country first. I shall notify Mr. Lincoln of this if he attempts to interfere with the sentence of any court ordered by me. If he wants an army, he must conform to the well-established rule of military actions, and not attempt to keep up the open rules of peace."

During World War I, early attempts by British correspondents to provide independent accounts of the fighting led first to the arrest and jailing of some and, eventually, to nearly complete censorship and the incorporation of reporters into the official war effort. For a time, American correspondents and those of other ostensibly neutral nations provided independent coverage, but with the United States entry into the war, Americans, too, were subject to censorship.

With Vietnam came a different kind of problem. An undeclared war, Vietnam was more foreign policy than national endeavor, and it was ultimately as foreign policy that a succession of administrations were forced to defend it. Right from the beginning it was a battle between government and the media. In 1963, President Kennedy's press secretary, Pierre Salinger, described reports of the failing U.S.-backed Diem government as "emotional and inaccurate."

Yet, for a number of years most correspondents supported the aims of United States policy in Vietnam. It was the effectiveness of the tactics used to carry out that policy that was criticized and commented upon. "We would have liked nothing better than to believe that the war was going well, and that it would eventually be won," *New York Times* correspondent David Halberstam later wrote of the early years of coverage, "but it was impossible to believe these things without denying the evidence of our senses."

As public and political criticism of the United States role in Vietnam began to grow in the late 1960s, government criticism of the media also grew. I would not argue for a minute that every news report from Vietnam was accurate and objective, or that the extensive use of television for the first time in a major conflict did not in many ways distort the story and shape public reaction to it in ways that are open to debate among reasonable people.

Journalists are no different from bankers or lawyers or auto mechanics or politicians. Some do their jobs well, others not so well. Some are honest and intelligent and courageous, others are ill informed and biased. Most are just trying to do a job.

What I argue for is rather a system, that, under our Constitution and traditions, permits, indeed demands, that the people of this country have access to all possible information that will enable them to have informed opinions, and make informed judgments on the policies of their elected leaders. And it is when the United States is involved in an overseas conflict as a function of the foreign policy of a particular administration, rather than as a nationally declared war, that the public most needs information.

Vietnam was our first modern example of reportage about war as foreign policy. And I would maintain that it was the policy itself, rather than the reporting of it, that ultimately lost the support of the congressional majority and the public.

Grenada, therefore, is the logical extension of an administration's understandable attempt to control and manage information about a policy, and therefore promote public and political support for it. Unlike the situation in the waning days of Vietnam, there is strong evidence that the Grenada policy has been widely supported by the public, and there is every reason to believe that, had independent coverage of the invasion been permitted, the public would still have backed it.

But political leaders and a military institution brought up with tightly controlled press coverage of World War II and offended by unfettered coverage of Vietnam are not in the mood to take chances. Moreover, as Secretary Shultz's statement reflects, the current administration—like General Sherman before it—has interpreted press criticism and questioning of its depiction of events in some areas as reason for doubt as to whether the American press is "on our side" or, by implication, the side of the enemy.

Nowhere has this suspicion been more evident than in government reaction to ongoing press coverage of another undeclared war, that in Central America. Whatever lessons remained unlearned from Vietnam in terms of how public information can influence public opinion have been retaught in spades over Central America's various wars, United States involvement in them, and administration policy toward them.

Acknowledging questions about administration policy in Central America, President Reagan turned the issue around to place the questions squarely on the back of the media and its patriotism. In his address to a joint session of Congress in April, 1983, he noted that "In spite of, or maybe because of, a flurry of stories about places like Nicaragua and El Salvador and, yes, some concerted propaganda, many of us find it hard to believe we have a stake in problems involving those countries."

In a 1982 speech to the Organization of American States, President Reagan strongly implied that the information reaching both Europeans and Americans about the civil war in El Salvador was a distorted version of what in fact was going on there, which he described in very strong terms as "very simply" an effort by Cuban and Soviet-backed Marxist-Leninists to take over a legitimate government against the will of its people.

In a 1983 interview that appeared on the front page of the *Washington Post*, Faith Ryan Whittlesly, director of public liaison at the White House and of a public relations effort to promote Administration policy on Central America, said that the news media and major United States churches "have tried to portray what we think are the bad guys, the communists, as Robin Hoods . . . . And I think," she said, "that the confusion has been deliberate, and that accounts for some of the ignorance" that the Administration appears to believe is behind the lack of public support for its policies.

According to a wide range of opinion polls, the Administration is correct in assuming that a large portion of the public is ignorant about what is going on in Central America. But what is even more interesting is that, according to those same polls, those who have no knowledge of events in Central America seem to have the same opinions as those who are more informed. And although the vast majority agree with the Administration's assessment of the threat in Central America and who is responsible for it, they are strongly opposed to what the Administration is doing about it.

In a nationwide *Washington Post*–ABC news poll taken in March 1982, the vast majority of those questioned about El Salvador said they agreed with the Administration's assessment that Cuba was improperly interfering in Central America, that most Latin Americans were opposed to a Cuba-style government, and that establishment of a pro-communist government in El Salvador would endanger United States security. Sixty-five percent of those questioned were aware of the fact that the United States is backing the government, rather than the rebels, in El Salvador. The public was about evenly divided over whether the war itself at that time was important to U.S. national security. Hardly anyone (3 percent) said they felt people in El Salvador would be better off if the rebels would win the war. One-third said the people of El Salvador would be better off with a government victory, and 38 percent said they felt it wouldn't matter either way.

Yet, when asked what the United States should do in El Salvador, more than two-thirds of those questioned said that we should back neither the rebels nor the government, but rather that the United States should stay out altogether. Fifty-nine percent said all U.S. military advisers should be pulled out of El Salvador, and 72 percent said they disapproved of any increase in the amount of United States military assistance to El Salvador. Although most said they strongly disapproved of the use of United States ground forces in El Salvador, at least half of those who expressed an opinion said they did not believe the Reagan Administration was telling the truth when it said it had no intention of sending American soliders to fight there. Perhaps most astoundingly, more than half of those questioned said they would support those young men who refused to be drafted to fight in El Salvador.

According to a subsequent set of polls taken about one year later, in May of 1983, public opinion was, if anything, more convinced that things were the way the Administration said they were in Central America, but at the same time the American public had become even more opposed to United States involvement there.

When President Reagan created the Kissinger Commission in the summer of 1983 to study and report on problems in Central America, he asked it to come back with advice on "means of building a national consensus on a comprehensive United States policy for the region." Yet now that the commission has made its report, it seems that Administration policy is more at odds with public opinion than ever. In El Salvador, for example, the commission concluded that "the present levels of United States military aid are inadequate," and recommended "significantly increased levels of military aid as quickly as possible," despite the fact that 70 percent of the American public opposes any increase at all in military aid.

The report states that "widespread ignorance about the area in this country is an obstacle, indeed a danger . . . . For most people in the United States, [Central America] is *terra incognita*. Probably few of even the most educated could name all the countries of Central America and their capitals, much less recite much of their political and social backgrounds."

More recent polls show that to be the case. In a public opinion survey conducted by the ABC-*Washington Post* Poll, in early 1984, 38 percent of those questioned said they had read or heard about the fighting between the Sandinista government in Nicaragua and the rebels seeking to overthrow it. Yet, in that same survey, 23 percent said the United States is backing the rebels, and 27 percent said we were backing the Sandinista government.

Still, those who knew and those who did not know which side the United States is backing were in agreement on one thing—more than half of those questioned said they didn't think the United States should be involved on either side. What these polls have reflected, over and over again, is not that Americans are specifically opposed to Administration assessments of what is at stake in Central America, or have been influenced by much other than the Administration's description, but rather that they are fundamentally opposed to United States intervention in what they consider an issue of relatively minor importance and that, overall, they are opposed to large scale foreign aid expenditures,no matter where the money is spent.

According to political scientist Richard Scammon, who served on the commission, what is important about public opinion is not that it support the commission's recommendations, but that it not be actively opposed to them. For the program to be implemented, Scammon told ABC-*Washington Post* pollster Barry Sussman, it has to be "tolerated, if not approved, by public opinion."

Did the press influence what people thought about Vietnam? Of course it did. But I would maintain that the biggest influence on mainstream public opinion in this country, the reason why many Americans turned against the war, was the increasing numbers of draftees and the increasing numbers of casualties that began to affect even the smallest towns in this country. Until that point, most of the opposition was in Congress.

Is the Congress influenced by what it reads in the press about Central America? Of course it is. But I would maintain that the partisan nature of congressional opposition to what essentially is a partisan foreign policy is the key to approval or rejection of that policy, rather than anything the press might or might not say about the region.

The press did not create political division in this country over Central America. In fact, it is a division that long predated the current Administration, causing problems equally as great for President Carter, who labored for nearly nine months before gaining congressional approval of a slimmed down version of assistance he had requested for Nicaragua.

It is precisely because so much political division exists on the issue that I believe it is incumbent upon the press to present as full a picture of events in Central America as possible. The basic division, again, is not over the nature of the threat of the relative importance of the various actors in the region, but over what U.S. policy ought to be for dealing with it. And I would maintain that the American press is in a good postition to write about the personalities and the events and the Central American institutions that play a part in the conflicts of the region, perhaps a better position than they ever have been in to cover a foreign conflict.

For the first time in which the United States is a major, albeit in some cases indirect actor, the press has equal access to all sides. The countries involved are small, with relatively well-developed transportation and communications infrastructures.

There are many ways in which the countries of Central America are unlike Vietnam, and one is that they are well known to a number of experienced journalists who have worked there for many years. They know the geography, the history, the people, the language. The countries are close to the United States. The mainstream press can send a number of correspondents simultaneously to cover several countries and several sides to a conflict. The range of information provided is therefore broadened, to the vast benefit of the debate in this country.

Perhaps, most importantly, in a war where propaganda can be as important and influential as bullets, all sides—in El Salvador and in Nicaragua—are relatively open to the press. Unlike the case in Vietnam, where few journalists were able to establish direct contact with the other side, and some of those did not return, both the Salvadoran government and guerrillas and the Sandinista government and the guerrillas fighting against it all seem to welcome contact with the media and to seek it out.

As a result, the United States finds itself involved in a conflict where it does not control the flow of information. More importantly, the Administration finds itself engaged in a policy that has become a subject of debate. In order for our system to work the way it was intended, it is the media's job to help that debate be as informed as possible.

In many cases, in fact, it is the media that are doing the only on-scene reporting on what the policy is and how effective it has been. As battle lines are drawn in Central America, and as the United States becomes more of a participant in the conflicts there, it has become more difficult for U.S. officials to gather information in the field.

In El Salvador, United States civilian personnel are no longer allowed to travel outside the capital to look at where our aid is going, or how the war is progressing. Other than American military officials, who are prohibited from coming into any contact with actual combat, only journalists now travel throughout the countryside to look at the progress of land reform, at the ongoing political campaigns leading to elections, at the human rights situation, and at the battles themselves.

These are all subjects of integral importance to Administration policy and efforts to gain support for that policy. They are also subjects of some disagreement, not between the press and the government, but between proponents and opponents of the policy.

Similarly, in Nicaragua, it is the journalists who travel into combat zones with the U.S.-supported rebels, and who provide a look at the policies and activities of the Nicaraguan government.

The American public, and its elected officials, deserve to hear all sides. They need to know where our money is going, how successful our programs are, and what the various actors in Central America say about the conflicts there. In order to have an informed opinion, they need this information from as many sources as possible.

All sides in Central America have accused the American press of twisting the news, of operating out of a bias, of promoting one side or another. Although the left, of course, sees the media as useful, it is basically distrustful of what it considers a capitalist-based system beholden to its own government. When it considers news reports favorable to its cause, it praises the freedom of the American press. When it sees them as unfavorable, it scorns us for being part of the imperialist war machine.

At the same time, any United States administration finds the press useful when it is reporting what the government says. I agree with the Kissinger Commission that the more people know about what is going on in Central America, the more intelligent our policy will be. The message that the Administration wants to convey on any particular subject is certainly part of the information that the press must communicate to the public, and I think the current Administration makes as good use of that access as any other—better than most, in fact.

The job the press has to do overseas is no different from the job it has in our own country. Neither this nor any other administration would say that its flexibility in conducting policy was limited, for instance, if we wrote that conservation organizations were unhappy with the Interior Secretary. City councils do not generally complain if the press quotes others who are disputing their policy in certain areas or their version of events. It is only in foreign policy that this occurs, because such information is somehow perceived to be damaging to national security.

What is our responsibility in Central America? To send the best people we can find, whose experience, professional judgment, and capabilities are beyond question. We have an additional responsiblity to analyze our sources, to look at who is telling us what and for what purpose, and, to the extent that we can, to communicate that identity and purpose to our audience so that bits of information can be weighed against each other.

We make mistakes, and we should admit them. Our coverage is incomplete, and we should be aware of it. Neither the *Washington Post* or any other newspaper or television network has the entire picture. What each has is a part of the puzzle, and a part of the mix that goes into the public debate.

As General Dwight Eisenhower said, public opinion wins wars, and this country has never had difficulty fighting wars with the support of national consensus. Under our system, however, it is public debate that wins support for policy. And there is no basis for debate without information.

FOUR

The American Democracy in the Global Community: Federal and University Roles in the International Education Triad

Sven Groennings

Sven Groennings is former director of the Fund for the Improvement of Postsecondary Education, United States Department of Education, United States Department of Education. After receiving his Ph.D. in political science from Stanford in 1962, Dr. Groennings taught in the Department of Government at Indiana University, specializing in European politics and American foreign policy. He has been staff director for the Wednesday Group, consisting of twenty-eight members of the United States House of Representatives, and director of the policy planning staff of the Bureau of European Affairs at the State Department. He served as deputy director of the Office of Policy and Plans and then director of the Office of Public Affairs, both for the Bureau of Educational and Cultural Affairs at the Department of State. Just prior to becoming director of the fund, he was a professional staff member of the U.S. Senate Subcommittee on Education, Arts and Humanities, Committee on Labor and Human Resources.

One of the characteristics of the American democracy in the world community is that it speaks with many voices, and not only from the Congress. The President's executive agencies implement policy not by bureaucratic action alone, but also by cooperative arrangements with the private sector, which is the deep reserve of American wherewithal. The opportunity to present this paper at The American University, a private university celebrating the fiftieth anniversary of its College of Public and International Affairs, provides an occasion for illustration in a foreign and educational policy arena close to this institution and hundreds of others. It is an arena of little-realized but remarkably great complexity. I am referring to the federal and university roles in international education, and I will focus on those linkages for which the federal rationale is conceived with regard to national security considerations.

Whether the federal government and the nation's institutions of higher education should be partners in international education is a key issue settled affirmatively long ago. There has been a significant and multidimensional postwar departure from the past, contemporaneous with the new federal/university partnerships in scientific research and in extending access to postsecondary education. The fundamental programmatic dimensions of the relationship have been renewed repeatedly by congressional reauthorization with the support of the national security and higher education communities. In effect, most of the time the key issues have been refinements of the overall dimensions—shifting emphases within categories—and the reconciliation of differences in federal and university perspectives.

The need for federal programs flowed from the extraordinarily changed situation which followed World War II: the assumption of an American world leadership role, the coming of global confrontation and ideological competition, the creation of new nation-states in the wake of decolonization, the growing importance of international economic relationships, the advent of instantaneous mass communications and public diplomacy, and the increasing complexity of relationships with other countries. These changes were of a new kind, with new dimensions, and dangerous. They brought challenges in the realms of ideas and relationships. National security would require more than military capability, which alone could not build the desired peace and whose use would be a last resort. National security would also require the development of other, nonmilitary competencies and relationships.

In the nuclear age, we evolved our deterrence theory and capability with the triad of nuclear delivery systems: land-based, sea-based and airborne. Yet, also in the nuclear age, international understanding had to be improved. Communication had become quick while knowledge remained shallow, and misperception could be dangerous. Misperception had influenced the outbreak of World War I, Hitler's assumptions, and the Japanese decision at Pearl Harbor, and there were signs that misperception might be troublesome in Asia, the Middle East, Latin America,indeed globally. It became understood that in an era in which public opinion and psychological factors can have determining consequences, it is important to have accurate pictures in people's minds. Exposure is perhaps especially important if it is human nature not to like what we don't understand. There is need for better contacts, analysis, and teaching, and for more and wider-ranging expertise.

To meet new national interests, the federal government created, across a dozen years, another triad, a *triad of programs involving educators*:—the Fulbright Program of *international exchange* to build knowledge, understanding, and professional and institutional linkages, now administered by USIA; *technical and developmental assistance* programs to help with nation building, administered by the Agency for International Development (AID) and the Peace Corps; and the campus-based *foreign language and area study programs*, authorized first under Title VI of the National Defense Education Act and now under Title VI of the Higher Education Act and administered by the Department of Education—for the purpose of developing expertise and enhancing America's needed competencies for world affairs.

As the first triad aims at deterring, i.e., impeding by fear aggressive actions against us (the word "deterrence" comes from the root that gives us "terror"), the second triad aims at improving our foreign relations by improving our understanding of others and linking this nation in cooperative and friendly relations. We deter through fear, but the second triad builds knowledge, contacts, respect, admiration, and sympathy.

These two triads are postwar structures, but there were precedents for executive initiative. Theodore Roosevelt established our first international exchange program, the Boxer Indemnity Fund, with China. In his inaugural address, in the spirit of the Good Neighbor Policy, Herbert Hoover called for international exchange. Franklin Roosevelt began a program in Latin America, bringing the young Nelson

Rockefeller to Washington to head it. But the major structures followed the war, with new initiatives or programmatic emphases by Presidents of both parties. The Truman Administration launched the Point Four Program for technical assistance and the Fulbright Program, which operated originally on surplus currencies, and the Smith-Mundt Act expansion, which authorized federal appropriations for it. The Eisenhower Administration developed the NDEA, beginning the Title VI programs. The Kennedy era added the Peace Corps and the new Fulbright-Hays Act, which again expanded the Fulbright Program; it added the East-West Center. Lyndon Johnson inititated the International Education Act, ill-fated in the Vietnam era, but nonetheless an initiative. The Nixon/Ford years witnessed improvements in the Fulbright Program's management and the designation of Title XII universities associated with the new Board for International Food and Agricultural Development. President Carter established the National Commisson on Foreign Language and International Studies and restructured USIA to include educational affairs. The Reagan Administration has created the International Youth Exchange Initiative.

The rhetoric has changed from time to time. In the exchange field, for example, the context changed from "good neighbor" to "cold war crusade" to "interdependence." Yet in each changing context, international education was considered an important de facto foreign policy instrument. The exchange programs, for example, including the Reagan Initiative, are viewed as adding credence to our policy of building peace while serving as a projection of the foreign policy of an open society which can extend contacts not only governmentally but also by direct people-to-people contacts. They are thus the other side of our national security picture, the second triad aimed at building a structure for peace.

THE UNIVERSITY AS PARTNER

This broad policy context, in which federal missions are based on needs for international competencies and relationships, naturally called for the involvement of the universities. Any partnerships, of course, would have to meet not only federal needs but also the university's concern about advancing its own mission in ways which would preserve its autonomy and academic values.

There were bases for a natural partnership: international involvement is basic to the very idea of a university. A university must reach out to the rest of the world because its function is to probe and teach about the universe of phenomena and ideas. A university is universal in its intellectual and scientific concerns.

Indeed, America's universities have been of worldwide influence in the development of knowledge and curriculum. They serve as models of educational opportunity and excellence. They have been a magnet to foreigners, some 350,000 of whom are studying in the United States now, thereby providing this country an invisible export worth perhaps $2 billion a year. Since 1949 more than two million students from developing countries have studied here, and currently nearly half the students in the world who are studying outside their own country are studying here. At this university and many others, we have educated great numbers of foreign faculty members, professionals, and national leaders.

It has, of course, been a two-way street. The very idea of the American research university followed the German model. Many of our universities' Nobel Prize winners came from abroad to join our faculties. Some of our brightest academics and public servants were Rhodes Scholars, including Senator Fulbright, whose inspiration for the American exchange program stemmed from that experience. The numerous intellectuals who fled Nazi Germany gave new directions to our disciplines, affecting them profoundly and pushing them to the forefront.

From a national as well as a university perspective, the values which our institutions of higher education represent in the world are fundamentally important: freedom of thought, of inquiry, of communication, and of association. Everywhere they represent the American and universal interest in human rights. No other American institutions convey these values more effectively, and no other set of American institutions is more effectively linked to foreign aspirations for a better life.

Yet the American university was not very international in either focus or clientele before World War II. For its own educational relevance in this global age, it has needed to expand its international dimension, just as the American government has needed to do so. While the university has proceeded in this direction on its own, the federal government has helped it develop its specialized capabilities, including many this country would not have had without federal support, such as capabilities in Soviet-Asian languages which could never have been of much interest to the states. As a natural sequel, faculty members who benefited from federal support have contributed to the broader internationalization of the university.

The universities continue to seek federal support for this field of activity. The broadest new proposal is from Michael Sovern, president of Columbia University, where Dwight Eisenhower served as president and where a recent handsome gift has endowed the W. Averell Harriman Institute for Advanced Study of the Soviet Union. Sovern has devoted his entire 1982–1983 President's Annual Report to international studies at Columbia and in the nation. In it he states that "America should call upon her great universities in far greater measure to help advance world security and understanding" and calls for a National Endowment for International Studies.

PARADIGM SHIFT AND PARADOX

Today the universities are encountering harder times than in the recent past. In these years of financial difficulties, are the campuses now turning inward? Does international education have any momentum? Here we encounter both paradigm shift and paradox. In one dimension, as viewed from my position with the Fund for the Improvement of Postsecondary Education, it is evident that international education is one of the current areas of major innovative vision and thrust on the nation's campuses. There are four major and broadly encompassing beachheads of change that I see people thinking about today:

● First, whereas the business curriculum has lagged behind the development and promise of international business at a time when doing American business means doing business with the rest of the world, the universities, prodded by the new accreditation standards of the Amercian Assembly of Collegiate Schools of Business, are beginning, albeit slowly, to move toward expanding business students' understanding to include international economics, finance, marketing and export administration as well as worldwide business conditions and possibilities viewed in the light of politics, labor movements, and cultures. There are an increasing number of models of curriculum development. Curricular change is coming, and we can expect it to assist in preparing this country to increase our firms' participation in export-related activity and, hopefully, to help the country overcome its enormous and growing trade deficits.

• Second, whereas foreign language learning has been tied to written and literary traditions, oral proficiency testing is on the near horizon and is likely to contribute to revitalization, as are language study for special uses like business and the utilization of new learning technologies. The thrust is toward practical communicative competence. People will be learning a foreign language as a skill to be used, with the measurement of achievement moving from a semesters-passed criterion to one based on proficiency. Predictably, the establishment of such a system will have catalytic effects on curriculum development and evaluation, and on the design of teaching materials. Changing the scorekeeping will change the game. Beyond foreign languages, moreover, this development may spur new assessment approaches in other fields.

• Third, whereas today not one precollegiate teacher in twenty has taken any international, comparative, or intercultural course en route to certification, the purpose of education is more and more understood to be to prepare students for the world in which they will be living. Little can be more predictable than the quickening impact of the rest of the world on today's teenagers, who will be only in their early thirties as we enter the next century. Several leading schools of education are developing plans to increase the international content of pre-service teacher education. The internationalization of teacher education is slow, but it is on the horizon.

• Fourth, whereas the liberal arts curriculum traditionally has included international course offerings, the international dimension now is increasingly being integrated into the core of the curriculum. The increasingly accepted premise is that developments beyond our borders will affect most American lives and that global perspective is needed. It is apparent that internationalization is attractive to students because it enhances curricular relevance to their lives. It is attractive to the faculty as an approach to revitalization. It is also becoming attractive to institutions because it provides a thrust for curricular coherence and a larger sense of direction and because it offers potential linkage between the liberal arts colleges and the professional schools.

These changes are in the making, but will take time to become common. Already they add up to a broad agenda for development and to a paradigmatic change for international education: toward broad utility and general education and beyond elitism and the production of experts.

Yet, paradoxically, there are signs in our colleges and universities that the junior faculty will have less international experience than the generation it will be replacing. The overseas experiences which in large part sparked on-campus developments are in contraction. Foundations send fewer people abroad. Junior faculty members are reluctant to become Fulbright Scholars or otherwise work abroad in an era involving sacrifices for working spouses, and there is real concern that the positions of those absent and untenured might be especially insecure in a tight and economizing academic market. Perhaps there is less fervor of mission among the junior faculty than among those who sought to build a different, better world after World War II. There is hard evidence that the cadre of university scientists who were involved in AID's development programs in the 1950s and 1960s is approaching retirement age and is not being replaced. So there are signs of reparochialization at the very time we are moving forward.

THE TRIAD

In the context of the changing American university, we come to the triad of federal programs at the nexus of foreign affairs and education. They are, as you will recall, foreign language and area studies, international exchange, and technical and developmental assistance.

The elements of the triad have distinct structures and histories, yet at their best they are mutually reinforcing, and they can contribute in complementary ways to the advancement of education and our foreign affairs capabilities. The issues involved are different but in each case are essentially generic and therefore enduring, and in each case they are the kind of implementational issues associated with the executive agencies more than with the Congress.

TITLE VI

Let us look first at Title VI. The core of any university's capability for service to the foreign affairs community is the expertise of its faculty. I suppose, although some strategic thinkers and some agriculturalists may have other views, that the core expertise needed is foreign language and area studies. The original Title VI premise, as stated in 1958, is that the nations needs "trained manpower of sufficient quality and quantity to meet the national defense needs of the United States." Title VI provides support for approximately 90 centers, funded and renewed on a competitive basis within a budget framework of around $20 million in most recent years. Most of the centers focus on world areas. Overwhelmingly the money supporting the centers is the universities', not the federal government's, but typically it was the federal spark, and that of the foundations, that led to the centers' establishment. Federal support has provided status, the margin of excellence, and the drawing power for other funding, while the Foreign Language and Area Studies (FLAS) fellowships have attracted the top students.

The typical student today, after his or her undergraduate years, gains foreign language competence and experience overseas and undertakes an interdisciplinary program within the center while earning a Ph.D. in an academic discipline. The graduates are employed mainly by the foreign affairs community, the national security agencies, international broadcasting services, business, and the universities, where they undertake analytic work, teach, and are available for consultation. Frequently, when dramatic events occur abroad, the centers' personnel are called upon to provide backround information to the press and educational institutions as well as to the government.

Title VI is the only program in the Department of Education having a direct and congressionally-defined national security rationale. In 1980 the Congress moved the authorization from NDEA to the Higher Education Act. In doing so, while removing "Defense" from the title, it reaffirmed the national security rationale, but it indicated that the time had come for the international dimension to be viewed as an integral part of federal higher education legislation, rather than as something apart. It also added Part B, a small dollar-for-dollar matching program to help prepare people for export-related activities. This additional thrust for title VI has offered a bright prospect for creativity and reinvigoration of programs traditionally separate on the campuses, bringing international economic and business perspectives into juxtaposition with the old NDEA programs. Thereby it added an economic rationale to that of national security for the Title VI program, and the program gained a broader constituency and purpose.

As one looks back across the years, one finds the issues within the Title VI category fundamentally the same. The generic issues are basically the following, and in some cases underlying them is perhaps the most difficult of all questions—namely, how does one answer these questions? Here they are:

- How many people are needed in which categories? For federal needs or broader needs? Calculated on what basis other than the previous year's base? How does one define geographic sufficiency?

- What particular competencies are needed? Competencies for what purposes and at what levels? Foreign language? Country or topical expertise? Practical competencies such as those related to exporting? Combined competencies? Assuming attrition of skills and that once-an-expert-is-not-always-an-expert, how do we maintain and upgrade the skills of the people we have trained? Is part of the problem how to match their skills to relevant employment?

- What should be the division of emphasis between foreign language and area studies? Between sharp, in-depth focus versus breadth? Between support for the centers and for student fellowships? Between predoctoral and postdoctoral fellows? Between national versus regional centers? Between focusing the money on flagship institutions versus encouraging the participation of other kinds of postsecondary institutions?

- To what extent should Title VI centers undertake outreach, diffusing international knowledge? What about citizen or lay competencies and the need for informed citizens who see relationships? Who in society does not need such exposure and should the federal government help with that and, if so, in what way?

This room full of people, like almost any other, will include a variety of answers to these questions for two reasons. First, you will assign different priorities to different world areas according to different criteria—for example, sense of basic importance versus growing importance versus current crisis versus the need to fill in the gaps. Second, the assessment of needs is an uncertain occupation involving assumptions about contingencies and margins of safety.

INTERNATIONAL EXCHANGE

Whereas the campus-based Title VI programs focus on international substance and promoting needed competencies, the Fulbright Program is in a sense far broader, having expanded to include 120 countries and spanning the full range of academic disciplines. It is an instrument of our public diplomacy and indeed of the diplomacy of the participating countries. It has enabled more than 50,000 Americans to study and teach abroad and more than 97,000 foreigners to study and teach in this country. It now involves, in all categories of exchange, 5,000 American and foreign citizens annually.

The Fulbright Program is the largest of USIA's educational and cultural exchange programs. Two-thirds of USIA's budget for these activities, which in fiscal year 1984 was nearly $93 million, supports the Fulbright Program. Most of the remainder supports international visitor programs, performances, and lectures.

In diplomacy, exchange is a vehicle for building understanding. It was important after World War II in reaching out to wartime enemies as well as allies, including building democratic understanding among German youth. As in the case of "ping-pong" diplomacy with China, exchange sometimes precedes diplomatic relations and serves as a communications link even when there are no formal diplomatic relations. I once heard Finland's President Kekkonen praise the Fulbright Program for its contributions to his country's renewal after the War. Third World countries similarly want its potential for developing capabilities and contacts. It seems that nearly all countries wish the status associated with the Fulbright Program and would consider it a diplomatic affront to be dropped. The age of interdependence, in which more decisions will be made internationally within more substantive areas, provides revitalized rationale for exchange as providing steps toward trust and cooperation among those who directly or indirectly will shape decisions. Renewed rationale has been provided also by the worldwide revolution of access to higher education; while postsecondary enrollment within the United States has doubled in the last fifteen years, it has expanded even more rapidly in many other countries, thereby vastly changing the nature of communications in those countries.

Internationally, the program is important because it respresents communication of high quality: in-depth, personal, involving dialogue, not viewed as propaganda, a builder of expertise and long-term professional and institutional relationships. It builds and connects communities of interest. It reaches foreigners of strong academic and leadership potential. It underscores mutuality: we teach and we learn, and of course we are more credible in our own classrooms when we actually have seen. The program has multiplier effects, because teachers have audiences and keep on teaching. It sacrifices no value associated with the university, while it enlarges the institutional capability and the meaning of the university. We gain knowledge, and not only knowledge about other societies: not long ago two-thirds of the world's science was in America, but now two-thirds is abroad. The program also induces some economic advantages, as those educated with American equipment have been known to cause the buying of American equipment. But more important is the result that we and others perceive one another more accurately. On a worldwide scale there has never been an exchange program more helpful than the Fulbright Program in promoting accurate perception, analysis, and teaching.

In forty-three countries, responsiblity for program operations is in the hands of binational commissions established by executive agreements between the United States and the host country. Those commissions also provide counseling services to students interested in studying in the United States. Twenty-eight countries share the cost, together contributing some $10 million in real money plus indirect subsidies. Our Board of Foreign Scholarships (BFS) establishes the broad policy guidelines. Under contract with USIA, several private organizations serve as implementing agencies and select the exchanges, among them the Institute of International Education; the Council for International Exchange of Scholars, which is affiliated with the American Council on Education; and, for the Soviet Union and Eastern European countries, the International Research and Exchanges Board of the American Council of Learned Societies. In 1979 there was added the Hubert H. Humphrey North-South Fellowship Program for mid-career professionals from developing countries.

In this very broad context, the 66 percent reduction in educational and cultural exchanges proposed for fiscal year 1982 brought quick reaction, including Senate testimony by former Fulbrighter Dr. Hildegarde Hamm-Bruecher, state secretary of the German Foreign Ministry. One result was the Pell Amendment to USIA's fiscal year 1983 authorization legislation to double, through annual increases, the size of the 1982 budget for exchanges, by fiscal year 1986. Clearly there is a continuing commitment to educational and cultural exchange programs, all of which, including Fulbright Awards, are in the same appropriation.

A new initiative has been proposed. In its report to President Reagan, the National Bipartisan Commission on Central America chaired by Henry Kissinger recommended the creation of a national scholarship program to bring to the United States as many as 10,000 students from Caribbean and Latin American countries in order to help counter Soviet and Cuban influence in this region. Discussion includes consideration of whether any program should be two-way and whether exchange should be entirely at the unversity level.

As observers of exchange programs, you might want to bear in mind that program stability has been affected not only by appropriations levels but also by variations in exchange rates, inflation differentials, extension of the program to a greater number of countries, foreign contributions, and even, on occasion, changes in the broader foreign policy framework. This is a complex field of activity.

There are some generic issues which have recurred repeatedly and which presumably any observer will also find surfacing in the future:

• What should be the relationship of educational and cultural programs to broader foreign policy considerations? Should they be an element of stability in relationships or of diplomatic leadership? Can constituency support and program effectiveness be maintained if they are viewed as politicized?

• Do we consider ourselves in exchange competition with the Soviet Union, which now funds nearly as many exchanges with Latin America as we do with the entire world? How do we add to the equation the quantities and qualities of the overwhelming proportion of foreign students who are in this country without federal support?

• What should be the relative emphasis upon the various components of educational and cultural programs or various audiences? For example, what emphasis should be placed on the exchange of people versus building institutions such as the American Studies Center in Warsaw? What emphasis on cultural performances, e.g., by symphonies or athletic groups, or on fine arts exhibits? On short-term topical lecturers rather than on scholars in residence? On reaching Europe's new generation of political and intellectual leaders?

• Which geographic areas and countries should receive what kind of programs? Should overall program resources be realigned to reflect the growing importance of developing countries? How can that be done, given established relationships and shared funding with the many "developed" countries with which we share binational commissions? Conversely, how can program cuts not primarily affect developing countries? How do we decide to have "a presence" rather than "a concentration" in a particular country? What weight do we place upon securing appointments for social scientists in Eastern Europe and what trade-offs are to be negotiated?

• What emphasis should be placed on academic exchange versus exchange of other professionals, e.g., journalists, or emerging political leaders coming under the International Visitors Program?

• What should be the mix of American faculty and students going abroad and foreign scholars coming to the United States? What critical mass is needed in any particular country to attract the best candidates and assure program prestige? What mix of foreign grantees should be assigned to what mix of American postsecondary institutions?

• What levels of academic appointment should be made, what proportions of senior lecturers versus research scholars, doctoral candidates, and teachers? How does one make these judgements in light of wanting to maintain program quality and prestige? What stipends are required to attract appropriate candidates?

• How can the Fulbright experience be made optimal for the scholar and most effective for the program? Should scholars be made available to a region or to a single university? What should be the length of stay? How do we overcome foreign language deficiencies among the applicants, U.S. and foreign, so that we can better match candidates with country requests for people in certain fields?

• How can the government best complement private sector programs, especially in youth exchange?

• How is program effectiveness to be evaluated?

• Can new methods of assuring financial support be devised, e.g., utilizing a share of economic development soft currency loan repayments or tapping private sector funds overseas? (Recently the first method has also been mentioned in connection with Title VI.[1])

These have become standard issues. Across the years, officials in Washington and in more than a hundred of our embassies have expressed a variety of broad and very particular perspectives, as have some academics. As observers of this field of endeavor, you are similarly likely to have a variety of answers to these enduring issues.

DEVELOPMENT ASSISTANCE

The third element of the triad is development assistance, involving the universities in contractual relationships to undertake projects in developing countries for AID.

Activities began after President Truman, in Point Four of his inaugural address, promised to share technological knowledge with developing nations. John Hannah, then president of the National Association of State Universities and Land-Grant Colleges, said his institutions would help. These were the universities which had spear-

---

[1]The National Advisory Board on International Education Programs, which is a creation of Title VI and is chaired by University of South Carolina President James Holderman, has issued a report, *Critical Needs in International Education* (1983), calling for a national fund which should receive "part of the reflow of funds generated by the overseas sale of U.S. government military and other properties, and by interest payments on overseas technical assistance loans." For many years P.L. 480 foreign currencies earned from U.S. surplus agricultural sales abroad have been used to support international exchange, but little remains of this source of funds.

headed our own agricultural development, and they remain the primary AID contract universities, instrumental, for example, in the "green revolution."

The early focus was on building foreign institutional capabilities, as in the best-known example of India. In 1949, India's University Education Commission recommended the establishment of a new system of rural universities which would provide education for production, a major conceptual departure from tradition. In a twenty-year period six American universities, each working in a different region of India yet coordinated through a Council of United States Universities for Rural Development in India and all collaborating with the Ford and Rockefeller Foundations, helped to establish the first nine agricultural universities in India. They contributed 700 people-years by 300 staff members while receiving more than 1,000 Indian faculty members and graduate students for study on their six campuses. In India they contributed to the development of new varieties of rice, wheat, and cotton and many new programs. Our faculty advanced new concepts of teaching, research, extension service, and management, while they benefited from their experience for their own renewal and teaching. That is an easy model to keep in mind. It was to change.

The leeriness toward international involvements caused by the Vietnam experience contributed to reconceptualization. In 1973 Congress provided the "New Directions" mandate, directed at the poorest of the poor, toward crop production and resources productivity and away from building dams, roads, and institutions, away from developing human capital and idigenous institutional capacity—the activities best suited to university action. However, some countries needing less infrastructure support sought more scientific and technological development.

The "New Directions" mandate produced a reaction. A major upgrading of the university role began in 1975 with the addition of Title XII, "Famine Relief and Freedom from Hunger," to the Foreign Assistance Act of 1961. Title XII pulls together many of the university-related components of AID's programs. It is popular with the universities because of its conceptual and operational changes: it engages the universities in baseline studies of host country capacities and needs so that assignments can be analyzed in the context of the whole development of educational and human resouces; it involves preselection of the implementing university, which then designs the project collaboratively with the host country, it provides assistance to our universities to expand their internationally oriented capacities for institution-building and research as part of development assistance in agriculture, including assistance to strengthen our small and minority institutions so that AID can draw upon a broader range of resources; and it includes funding for long-term collaborative research between American and foreign institutions on food production, distribution, storage, marketing, and consumption.

Also, it provides a now very active Board for International Food and Agricultural Development (BIFAD), which provides overall advice to AID's director. Of course, there are degrees of implementation. The current AID administrator, Peter McPherson, is a former member of BIFAD and has been encouraging the development of more effective cooperation between AID and the approximately 140 Title XII universities.

It is still the case, nonetheless, that the universities have a limited capability to respond to AID program needs. There are shortages of technical skills and in language and area studies preparation, and structural barriers as well. Those are university shortcomings in the partnership. Most of the enduring issues of this leg of the triad are partnership issues:

• The core issue is: how can this country mobilize more systematically the resources of United States agricultural universities on behalf of the rural poor in the developing countries?

• What can AID, which sometimes operates within a volatile U.S. official relationship with particular countries, do to increase and strengthen university and faculty incentives for deeper commitment and more systematic involvement? Can AID, which controls the finances, make long-term commitments to projects and offer enough pay to compensate for career detours and the lack of glamour in some posts? As an inducement, can it assure research opportunities in the disciplines or in the field of development?

• What should be AID's emphasis upon the long-term institution-building programs and baseline studies which are most attractive for university participation?

• What can the universities do to make overseas activity an integral part of university life, work, and responsiblities? More specifically,

what can the universities do to ease the internal constraints on participation caused by their own appointment, promotion and tenure policies
and how, for promotion and tenure, will they evaluate performance in
an international setting?

• How can the universities make available the number of personnel
needed for overseas assignments without being stuck with commitments
to people they otherwise would not have hired? Can they do it
consortially? Given the increased age of their faculty participants, what
can they do to encourage the overseas experience of young faculty?

• What can be done to overcome deficiencies in the agricultural universities' substantive capability to respond to AID program needs: the
common inadequacies of foreign language skills especially, the lack of
area and cultural understanding, the lag in up-dating and revitalizing
professional preparation programs on Third World development? Can
Title VI programs include more development content and be better
linked to AID program needs?

• Especially in a time of retrenchment and strong domestic focus,
there is also a state-level issue: to what extent should and can the
international aspect of public service be a function of state land-grant
universities? To what extent is this aspect a proper part of the international dimension of the university?

• What mechanisms can be devised to assure stability of the AID-
university relationship, given the basic problem of reconciling AID
"country plan" objectives with university concerns about their own
missions and faculty interests? To what extent should faculty experts be
involved in project design and modification?

• As some countries begin to need collaborative relationships more
than unilateral aid, how can AID respond? What mechanisms for continuing relationships might be developed with AID graduate countries
no longer receiving aid, e.g., Brazil, Mexico, Venezuela, Nigeria, Tai-
wan, and Korea? Can experts from their universities and ours work
jointly on problems in other countries? Can we cooperate with other
providers of aid?

TRIAD DIMENSIONS

It is the AID programs that are the largest financially in the
federal-university international relationship, as they add up to some

$250 million per year within Title XII and perhaps as much as $100 million in other segments of the AID domain. The triad as a whole involves minimally $400 million of federal commitment. I am not including sums for foreign affairs research, such as the $5 million recently authorized under the Lugar-Biden Amendment for the State Department's Bureau of Intelligence and Research to undertake Soviet studies; such work tends to be short term and has not been heavily funded. This kind of money usually flows to institutions associated with Title VI capabilities.

While my framework is limited today to the "Big Three" of the federal-university international relationship, I would like to indicate that there are several other federal programs which include aspects of international education and in some way involve or influence universities. The staffs of the Foreign Service Institute and the Defense Language Institute are part of the professional international studies community and have had great influnece upon the study of foreign languages and the assessment of proficiency. While the number of people involved has not been great, perhaps 100 universities have been involved in interchange authorized under the National Science Foundation Act. I have not included the $108 million budget for the Peace Corps, whose 100,000 returned volunteers have provided more than 65,000 classroom/work years in developing countries. The Peace Corps is largely not involved with universities, although some training occurs on our campuses and many volunteers return to graduate school. Also, I am not including the two massive learning programs associated with the military, as they are either not on campuses or not primarily international—namely, the International Military Education and Training Program, which since 1950 has provided training in the United States and abroad in 2,000 different specialties for more than 500,000 foreign military personnel from more than 100 countries, and in-service (non-ROTC) tuition assistance programs currently involving 650,000 enrollments in several hundred colleges and universities in the United States and abroad, including, for example, students in the overseas programs of the University of Maryland and the University of Southern California. Again, my framework has been limited to the "Big Three" of the federal-university relationship.

CONGRUENCE OF DIRECTION

The universities are more inclined than is the federal government to view the various aspects of international education as one administrative domain and to contemplate their relationships, whereas for reasons of history and policy context the federal government divides its jurisdictions across different congressional committees and administrative agencies.

Notably, however, USIA and AID are developing a broad cooperative relationship which will produce improved USIA coverage of U.S. economic assistance programs, beginning in Africa. The two agencies have exchanged personnel to assist administrators in developing the program.

The thrust for international substance, including contractual service, has been influencing university structures. It has become desirable to have a central and holistic view of the triad elements on campus (as well as any overseas campuses, study-abroad programs, and overseas fund-raising) plus arrangements for foreign students, whose presence in this country raises still other issues of federal policy, especially regarding visas. Also, international programs increasingly encompass component departments and colleges, among them business schools, schools of education, and colleges of arts and sciences, agriculture and health. The universities are now commonly discussing the desirability of deans or vice-presidents for international affairs in order to focus the commitment, energies, and priorities of the institutions.

One might hazard the prediction that the international dimension on campus will grow with the growth of technology, which already has made the world smaller. It is in technology that economic growth is most prominent and international competition the greatest. The more technological our society becomes, the larger will be the international share of the economy and the more we will be dealing with the rest of the world. It may well be this international development that will enable the bridging of C.P. Snow's two cultures, the scientific/technological and the liberal arts.

Predictably, the federal involvement with the academic community in the international domain will continue, to the extent that earlier assumptions continue to be considered valid. In summary, these have been:

  • First, that foreign policy concerns are of fundamental and growing importance and involve increasingly complex relationships with other countries;

  • Second, that our national security requires very special expertise;

  • Third, that our foreign policy objectives will include building respect, trust, and enduring cooperative relationships and that achieving these objectives will require in-depth international communications as part of our public diplomacy; and

  • Fourth, that educational institutions play a crucially important part not only in preparing this country for a world of change but also in communicating with the rest of the world and building the kinds of positive, long-term relationships which are among our foreign policy objectives.

The context in which we are meeting is one of celebrating the last fifty years of concern with public service at this private university and anticipating the next. No issue is likely to be more important than national security. We can expect to face two kinds of questions: how to assure deterrence and how to improve our foreign relations. Each area has its triad. I encourage your constructive thought about the linkage between education and our foreign relations. In this domain, the university can have a very positive impact on the world in which we all live.

FIVE

The Role of the Government in International Education: The Next Fifty Years

Gale W. McGee

*Gale W. McGee is a former United States Senator from Wyoming and a for-
mer United States ambassador to the Organization of American States. As Senator, he served on the Foreign Relations Committee from 1958 to 1977 and as a
member of the United States delegation to the twenty-seventh General Assembly of
the United Nations. He received his Ph.D. from the University of Chicago in
1947. He has taught history at Nebraska Wesleyan, Iowa State College, Notre
Dame, the University of Chicago, and the University of Wyoming. At Wyoming
he was also the director of the Institute for International Affairs.*

"Europe's distresses spelled America's successes" was the punch
line in a small volume that my major professor of history at the University of Chicago always used to open his course in diplomatic
history.[1]

The strife of Europe indeed had afforded openings in diplomacy
which the United States had exploited well during its first century and
a half. World War I, however, became a catalyst, but not until the
Americans had first enjoyed the luxury of hesitation and delay while
the powers in Europe were slowly bleeding to death. Ending up in the
ranks of the victorious allies, the United States for the first time in its

---

[1] J. Fred Rippy, *America and the Strife of Europe*, University of Chicago Press, 1938.

history became a participant as one of the major powers in the world consigned to the responsibilities of peacemaking.

In a sense, World War II began as a repeat performance. Once again the American people hesitated, procrastinated, and delayed— spared by the strife of Europe from having to make the tough decision on war or peace. It took the Japanese attack at Pearl Harbor to shock the badly divided American public into closing ranks once again.

But World War II destroyed for the Americans the luxury of choosing between two sides in the politics of the world. Being one of the giants of the earth, the United States had at once to sort out, with little delay, its priorities and its options. Called into question at the very outset had to be the United States' system of responsibility for making foreign policy. Under the Constitution, policy was vested heavily in the President, with the Senate giving advice and consent, ratifying treaties, and with the two houses reserving the power jointly to declare war.

But what will the realities of the remainder of this century and beyond require? We meet here at The American University to examine the foreign policy requisites for our country in the global community of the next fifty years. I propose to examine in particular those factors relating to the respective roles of the President and the Senate in U.S. foreign policy.

What Pearl Harbor had done to the previously isolationist generations of the 1930s and the 1940s, victory in the Atlantic and the Pacific ending World War II achieved through a strong bipartisanship among the American people, as they assumed for the first time their responsibilities in world power. A notable series of world events descended upon Americans in rapid succession, the first being the creation of the United Nations, an international body which sought to correct or adjust the limitations of the old League of Nations. The hopeful dreams of its founders were necessarily watered down to accommodate the two giants of the world, the Union of Soviet Socialist Republics and the United States of America. Even so, as fifty-one nations signed on, they also agreed on basing it in New York City—a perceptual contrast to the "neutral" ground which supported the old League of Nations in Geneva. Hardly was the ink dry on the signatures of those who signed the U.N. charter, however, when the rumblings and threats reflecting the strains between the United States and the Soviet Union at San Francisco threatened the peace.

The United States had a curious, if brief, experience with its idyllic hopes for a world at peace. An American military mobilization of more than twelve million by the end of the war was immediately demobilized; an America which had escaped the devastation heaped upon Britain, Germany, and Japan offered massive economic assistance not only to its allies but to the vanquished as well. Offers to the Soviets, however, were declined; even unofficial offers to share a short-lived monolopy on atomic know-how were greeted with "nyet."

The creation of the United Nations was almost immediately cast against the threatening backdrop of the cold war. From the Truman Doctrine of 1947, which sealed off Turkey from Soviet tampering, through the Berlin Airlift in 1948, the China White Paper of 1949, the war in Korea in 1950, the confrontation in Cuba in 1962, and ending finally by the mid-1960s in Vietnam, the strains of cold war severely taxed diplomatic relations between the two great powers.

It was Winston Churchill who noted during the Berlin Airlift crisis that "If you Americans had acted this time as you did after the First World War, Russia would be on the Atlantic Coast of Europe tonight." It was an approbrium applicable to the first two decades following World War II.

By the mid-1960s, the syndrome of cold war diplomacy had become commonplace: two Berlins, two Germanys, two Europes, two Koreas, two Chinas, and then two Vietnams—all of which epitomized a world divided. Shortly after his own traumatic diplomatic experiences in the Cuban crisis in 1962, Ambassador Adlai Stevenson summarized his discouragement: "One world was our dream, but two worlds are better than no worlds." The two-worlds syndrome had a considerable influence on the rationalizations of American leaders during the Vietnam crisis.

In a sense, the bipartisanship so characteristic following World War II was strongly reflective of Stevenson's two-worlds rationalization. Its strength rested heavily upon the common experiences of an entire generation of Americans who had shared a worldwide two-front war and had waged a tough series of wars and near wars together. That bipartisan generation managed successfully to bridge the rising differences between the president of the United States and Congress, particularly in foreign policy.

Two events, however—Vietnam and Watergate—exposed potentially grave weaknesses in our constitutional foreign policy structure as well as in policy procedures. The national trauma which both events evoked shattered much of the spirit of the bipartisanship so characteristic of the first two decades after the war. In particular, the roles of the president and the Senate were called into question. Given the nature of the world around us, and in particular because of the increasing capability of humanity to destroy itself, it is important that we resolve the extremes of the adversary relationship between the legislative and the executive branches of our government.

The core of our problem has been put well by Warren Christopher, deputy secretary of state during the Carter Administration. He has written that "Our basic need is to reconcile the imperatives of democracy at home with the demands of leadership in the world."

Many distinguished and experienced Americans are devoting a substantive amount of time to this question. Some have already concluded that another system of government may be required, perhaps a parliamentary type. Others contend that basic structural changes are needed which would require new amendments to the Constitution, such as limiting the president to a single six-year term. Another proposal would extend House terms to three or four years, another would limit senators to two terms, and yet another would form an international union among the Atlantic democracies.

But there are also many scholars (including this writer) who tremble at the thought of tampering with the Constitution on such matters, fearing, as many do, that it could lend itself to a serious unraveling of the constitutional fabric. Others point to the flourishing of single-issue groups, each with their own vision of new constitutional conventions and a new system which would appear to be laden with similar problems.

I for one do not believe we need to hold a new constitutional convention, nor ought we to resort to the amending processes to correct our foreign policy problems. We would be moving backward, moreover, were we to attempt an adjustment of presidential problems by transferring them to the 100 members of the United States Senate. Having served at both ends of Pennsylvania Avenue, I believe it is not too late to adjust the present mechanism from within, both at the presidential level as well as that of the Senate, at the same time preserving the principle of the separation of powers deeply implanted in the Constitution.

But if we are to succeed in changing our system from within, it is important that we not be tempted to reconstitute the terms of foreign policy responsibility even in the relatively recent image of the nostalgic 1950s. The world around us has changed in so many substantive ways since the bipartisanship of the Eisenhower years that to look backward at this point in time could seriously jeopardize our efforts to cope with the foreign policy requirements in the remainder of this century. The oft-used commencement reminder that while history can be an excellent guidepost it remains a poor hitching post is appropriate to our present search for wise, new foreign policy procedures as well as directions.

In the past two decades (1964–1984) substantive changes have occurred in the dimensions of world affairs that at the very least modify many of our assumptions of the 1950s, and at most render them inapplicable to the solution searches of the 1980s and 1990s. Herein I suggest four changes to illustrate the point:

• First, the successful launching of Sputnik by the Soviets in 1957. For a dozen years after World war II, the atomic factor remained off center stage due to the monopoly enjoyed by the United States. With the launching of Sputnik, the "moment of change" arrived, and our own population began to look for a place to hide.

To illustrate: In 1957 new to the campus of the University of Wyoming was a young couple from New Jersey who had literally studied geographical areas of the United States to escape "The Bomb." They found that spot near the Colorado-Wyoming border and began their careers anew at the University.

October 4, 1957, Sputnik was successfully launched.

December 13, 1957, the secretary of defense announced the location of the first intercontinental missile base at Cheyenne, Wyoming, approximately thirty-five miles east of this couple's new sanctuary.

January, 1958, they resigned and departed—we know not where. Literally, there was no place to hide. They had traveled from a target point in the New Jersey-New York area to a target point in the Wyoming-Colorado area. The nuclear war threat was "center stage," regardless of geographic location.

• A second change: the decline of bipartisanship. By the mid-1960s the World War II generation was growing old and tired and declining in numbers. Bipartisanship was soon displaced by "me first" and the weakening of political party attractiveness to the new generation. A substantive replacement of individual priorities was the result. By then, politics had become "dirty business," and government itself was a common enemy.

• A third change occurred in the ranks of the Third World countries. The new United Nations, with 51 members in 1946, had more than tripled those numbers by the 1980s to 157 (or even more perhaps by the time this script appears). The numbers were less important than the new perceptions of the younger nations.

The first generation of new leaders of the governments which were freed from the shackles of colonial rule, after World War II, generally leaned upon the metropoles from which they had split, especially for guidance and for structuring of their new modes of government—leaders like Jawaharlal Nehru in India, Kenyatta in Kenya, Houphuoet Buonet in Ivory Coast, William Tubman in Liberia, Kenneth Kaunda in Zambia, Charles Malik in Lebanon, Julius Nyerere of Tanzania, Lee Kuan Yew in Singapore, and Sukarno in Indonesia. Even Emperor Hailie Selassie of Ethiopia should occupy a niche with the above group. The dramatics of his resistance against the colonial rule of the Italian government of Mussolini became a forerunner to the anti-colonial crusades of the 1950s and 1960s.

In most of the above illustrations the United States was instrumental in pressuring the colonial powers of Europe to initiate steps toward granting independence to their former colonial outposts. Many of the new governments in turn looked to the American Declaration of Independence as a model for their own. While serving as chairman of the first African Subcommittee of the Senate Foreign Relations Committee in the U.S. Senate during the early 1960s, I had the occasion to meet personally with each of the African independence leaders listed above, and I can personally attest to their original independence motivations.

By the mid-1960s, however, the second generation of Third World leaders was already taking over from their own founding fathers, frequently by violent means, and in some cases moving to separate themselves even further from the old colonial nations of the first half of the twentieth century, as well as from the United States in particular.

By his second term, President Eisenhower had sensed the implications of this change. He was concerned that the escalating desires and expectations of the Third World would become a far more explosive factor in world politics than the earlier international communist party activities had been from the 1930s through the 1950s. The president warned that, unless or until the widening gap between the very richest nations and the poorest are meaningfully reduced, there could be no peace.

With the Group of 77, the North-South Dialogue, and the preponderance of Third World votes against the West in general and the United States in particular, the complexities of foreign policy decision making in Washington have increased considerably and very much in the vein predicted by "Ike."

• A fourth change since the 1950s is the dimension and character of news. Television and other communications technology have converted news gathering into the phenomenon of "instant news." The contrast from the days of nineteenth-century diplomacy is mind-boggling. At the beginning of that century, President Thomas Jefferson was exchanging letters with his predecessor and long-time friend, John Adams. The new president was filling Adams in on the state of foreign policy in 1801. Jefferson wrote that affairs with the British were still troubling: with France we were exploring new opportunities, but in regard to Spain, "We haven't heard from Pickering [the U.S. ambassador] in many months, so we conclude that matters are settling down in Madrid."

What a contrast with instant news today. Someone has suggested that had General Dwight Eisenhower had live TV coverage at Omaha Beach, it might have been difficult to hold public opinion on course. There's no doubt, in any case, that the problems of decision making in national and international politics have been seriously compounded by the new dimensions of coummunication, such as sensationalism, instant judgments, and even greater play on what goes wrong rather than what goes right.

With these factors in mind, the process of evaluating our constitutional procedures in foreign policy responsiblity remains complicated at the very least, and sometimes impossible to resolve at the very worst. The astute observations of three distinguished gentlemen capsulize the dimensions of the problem as well as the urgency of resolving it.

In the early 1800s Alexis de Tocqueville wrote: "I do not hesitate to say it is especially in the conduct of their foreign relations that democracies appear to be decidedly inferior to other governments."

Over a century and a half later Walter Lippmann, in a luncheon conversation with this writer, expressed deep concern over the state of public opinion. An impassioned opinion, he suggested, imposes "a compulsion to make mistakes," as a consequence of which, members of the U.S. Senate had been reduced to insecure and intimidated men.

Former Senator J. William Fulbright, distinguished former chairman of the Senate Foreign Relations Committee, wrote in *Foreign Affairs* (Spring, 1979) nearly two centuries after Tocqueville's observation, "I confess to increasingly serious misgivings about the ability of the Congress to play a constructive role in our foreign relations . . . "

In this monograph I do not choose to evaluate the options of systematic changes to another form of government (a parliamentary system, Atlantic Union, etc.) or even constitutional amendments to our present system, because they either would not meet the requirements of world leadership or would in other ways complicate rather than resolve our present problems. With procedural modifications at both ends of Pennsylvania Avenue, however, our present system would be better able to cope with foreseeable difficulties in meeting the requisites of world leadership.

Let us look first at the executive branch, the office of the president of the United States. The founding fathers, reflecting their sorry experiences as members of thirteen sovereignties, sought to vest foreign policy responsibilities in a single source. "Speaking with one voice" was a strongly felt requisite for the new government.

To the U.S. Senate was given the role of advice and consent. It is this relationship around which much of the controversy over responsibilities for foreign policy has centered. The president, it is asserted, too often notifies but fails to seek advice and consent. Senate critics want to be in on the take-off as well as the landing.

The president, on the other hand, is concerned about classified materials or diplomatic political delicacies that might unnecessarily strain relations with another government. For most executive documents and treaties there would be no such concern among the individual senators. But the few remaining instruments rightfully should bear close consultation, scrutiny, and the right of dissent or modification by the senators.

If the advise and consent process is to succeed, it requires the strongest good faith on both sides. The first rule for the president and his advisers is *never*—but *never*—try to deceive, run around, or lie to the Congress in an effort to avoid controversy. The outcome is always disaster, plus an intensified suspicion of the chief executive by the legislative branch that will carry over into unrelated matters. Where sensitivity of materials or the politics of the diplomacy is involved, the Senate and the White House often have worked out a formula for dealing with a small group of senators, bipartisan, senior in experience, etc. This congressional group in turn keeps other colleagues advised as required.

One last area remains which strains congressional-executive relations. The War Powers Act continues to fester amid the political rivalries at the two ends of Pennsylvania Avenue.

Enacted in 1973, the Act was motivated primarily by the efforts of President Richard Nixon to extend the Vietnam conflict into the neighboring reaches of Cambodia.

During the protracted floor debates on the Act, as a member of the Foreign Relations Committee I had a share of the floor management on the negative side. I opposed the measure as originally introduced by Senator Jack (Jacob) Javits of New York, primarily on grounds of historical precedent and experience and secondarily on some of its details.

The Senate's track record on such matters had been run only once before in the modern times of our republic—namely, between World War I and World War II. The modest dimensions of that conflict in terms of the limited time consumed and human and material costs would not ordinarily have signaled serious repercussions. Although only six senators voted against the World War I declaration in 1917, the Senate body quickly took over the unraveling of the Versailles Peace Conference. The upper body not only rejected the Peace Treaty, but blocked United States entry into the newborn League of Nations.

Worse still, in the 1930s, by which time our nation had divided itself into "Isolationists" and "Internationalists," the Senate enacted into law the Neutrality Acts of the 1930s. It was the motivation of those Acts which in hindsight caused so much concern about the leadership capabilities of the United States Senate. The thrust of these particular laws was to prevent World War II. They seriously hobbled the efforts of the government of the United States to cope significantly with the later Nazi threat under Hitler. Had it not been for the Japanese attack on Pearl Harbor, the consequences of the neutrality laws could have been even more disastrous.

During the War Powers Act debates of 1973 in the Senate, I felt dismayed at the direction it seemed to point—namely backward. The Act was motivated largely by the desire of many senators to prevent Vietnam. It was so precisely centered on the events of that era as to leave no other conclusion.

A few of us felt it could hobble rather than help efforts to adopt wise policies for the future. After a decade of living under the Act, those misgivings still linger. True, there have been some modifications to the War Powers legislation which have helped. But by the same token the increasingly sophisticated new dimension of war plus the shrinking of time and space leave in question the wisdom of the Act.

Are we once again busy with laws to prevent a conflict that occurred nearly two decades ago (yesterday's war, Vietnam) when most agree that new complexities since then require even greater initiatives by the president if we are to avoid yet another one? It is one thing to advise and consent, but it is quite another to hobble the presidency in time of crisis. Shortcomings in the White House are not corrected by transferring them to 100 secretaries of state in the Senate.

Nor are strained relations with the Congress the only area of executive problems. A second is the track record of hostilities between the president's cabinet chief on all foreign affairs, the secretary of state, and his personal adviser, the head of the president's National Security Council. While this issue did not arise during the Kennedy/Johnson years, it became conspicuous and embarrassing for Presidents Nixon and Carter. The struggle between Secretary of State William Rogers and Nixon's National Security Council chief Henry A. Kissinger, was a notable case in point. It was allowed to proceed much too far (and too long). Rogers was forced out, and Kissinger became secretary of state. But the point is that it shouldn't have been allowed in the first place. The secretary of state is the institutional person responsible to the president. The national security director is only privately the president's adviser. He is not subject to senatorial approval and thus should be confined to the role of *private* counselor to the president. Kissinger violated the role by "going public" through press conferences, media shows, and the like.

President Gerald R. Ford's Administration didn't experience the problem (Kissinger remained on as secretary of state), but President Jimmy Carter fell into the Nixon syndrome. Zbigniew Brzezinski, as Carter's national security chief, soon opened a barrage of verbiage challenging Secretary of State Cyrus P. Vance. The bombardment continued until Vance resigned his post late in the Carter years. Fortunately for the system, the National Security Council chief did not get Cy Vance's job, but much unneccessary confusion had already been injected into foreign policy problems during President Carter's regime.

Thus far under the Reagan Administration this question has remained in lower key, although it threatened to break out early on. Secretary of State Al Haig has written in his recent volume of the efforts of the president's Security Council adviser, Richard Allen, to challenge him in the post.[2] And other members of the Reagan White House staff apparently were involved in forcing Haig's resignation and replacing him with George Shultz.

Future administrations would do well to keep a tight rein on Security Council advisers vis-á-vis the new secretary of state. Such struggles are not only demeaning within our system; they send the wrong signals overseas.

A thoughtful add-on at this point would apply equally to the legislative and executive branches. It comes from Stanley Heginbotham of the Congressional Research Service. His suggestion would provide for an interchange of senior staff people at the Senate with senior staff in the executive branch, particularly in foreign policy areas. Too many times has one end of Pennsylvania Avenue failed to understand a signal or an opening for meaningful compromise sent by the other. The result has been unnecessary friction.

Now, to turn to the Senate. While we have been taking a look at the executive branch of our government, it is important to stress that

[2]Subsequently, however, the Reagan Administration has sought to clear up this matter. In an address to the Former Members of Congress organization in the Spring of 1984, the president's national security Adviser, Robert (Bud) McFarlane, made a strong statement of the president's intent to preserve the office of secretary of state as the responsible authority on foreign affairs and diplomacy. The national security adviser was to remain the President's private counselor but was to avoid public policy announcements and/or clashes with the secretary of state.

shortcomings of the White House should not tempt one to solve those problems by transferring them to the United States Senate. But there are changes in Senate procedures that would be helpful.

First, the Senate, by cleaning up its own house, has to become once again "leaderable." Majority Leader Howard Baker himself is the author of the term "unleaderable," which circumstance may be a substantial part of his motivation for wishing to give up his leadership post.

One of the explanations given for this leadership demise is that the Senate, after Watergate and Vietnam, may have overreformed itself. A complaint most commonly heard around the Senate floor points to the overstaffing of subcommittees in particular. Too many subcommittees have proliferated in recent years to the point that there aren't enough senatorial bodies to go around. (Some senators are on as many as sixteen or seventeen subcommittees.) Staffers multiply in proportion even as substance and depth have thinned considerably. One consequence has been a proliferation of legislative bills with a resultant glutting of the calendar by numbers alone. While there has always been a large number of innocuous or otherwise unimportant bills to be considered, the increased volume of minutia has cluttered the legislative processes.

Another factor contributing to the malaise of the Senate has been the rate of turnover bringing in more than the usual number of new senators. By 1982, for example, there were fifty-five senators in their first term! Lack of experience, and most surely a lesser sense of history, would have to account for some of the "unleaderability" of the upper body.

A third complication for Senate procedures is the television camera. Television coverage has extended the legislative processes somewhat, particularly in committee procedures. The number of individual speeches by committee members goes up in direct proportion to the presence of TV coverage. Moreover, the current practice of televising most committee processes compounds the problem. A committee mark-up, for example, may take double the ordinary time required. Politics, it has been said, is the art of compromise. But on camera it's another matter. With constituents (or worse, lobbyists supporting the individual member financially) filling the hearing room, it becomes an unreality to expect a particular senator or senators to compromise their *public* commitments while their public watches them on the TV screen.

The committee member often has to make one speech for "the folks out there." Then the committee meets in someone's office or back room to do battle in private over acceptable compromises or just plain hard bargaining. Once the basic compromise is worked out, they then go public one more time merely to confirm what has been achieved off camera.

In my travels to various campuses to speak on these questions, someone always can be counted on to raise the question "What would Lyndon Johnson and Everett Dirksen have done with this problem? They were strong leaders." The answer is that, with the present conditions and procedures being what they are, it is doubtful whether even they could have led.

There is one more adjustment in the Senate system that should be undertaken without delay—namely, a greater use of the staggered, six-year term concept for senators. At the founding of the republic, senators were given six-year terms, with one-third placed in office each two years. The purpose was clear. With longer terms they could be protected against the day-to-day whims of the populace in general, and with only one-third of the senators running for office every two years, the remaining two-thirds could become the steadying hand on the rudder of the ship of state. In recent years, at least, this concept has been neglected, and some argue it actually may have been destroyed.

Most surely it has been neglected, but hopefully, it still can be restored. Because of its place as one of the foundation stones in the foreign policy concepts of our republic, its revivability constitutes a strong potential leglislative base for refurbishing the Senate's constitutional role in foreign policy. Assuming, as we must, the Senate's determination to clean up its act, as one of its critics has written, the new Senate must turn meaningfully to the task of utilizing to the fullest extent the staggered terms of its membership.

Four sectors of the United States Senate need to be brought into a common focus on the problem: the Senate leadership, the Senate Rules Committee, the party caucuses, and the senators as individually elected officeholders.

Obviously the first priority is that the Senate recover and reestablish its own leaderability. Both institutional proceedings and "senatorial courtesies" need refurbishing. It is important that this begin now rather than later as some have suggested. The present-day Republican and Democratic leadership positions are held by senators of long experience. Their sense of history is an invaluable asset for a new beginning. In addition, each understands the many interlacings that hold "The Club" together. Both can speak with a strong voice as to the urgency of the problem of creating a new leaderability. Both are skilled partisans as well as expert practitioners in bipartisanship. Each has long experience in "keeping books" (favors extended, due bills that can be collected) and a deep sense of the variables among their individual colleagues. It is important that the two leaders move without delay, for they have both lived through the extended transition of the Senate into unleaderability. Their combined experience should be irreplacable in restoring the Senate to a more significant and responsible role in advice and consent.

The Rules Committee is even now, as I understand, working on procedural guide lines for the future. Reducing the numbers of committess and subcommittees should be high on their list. Tightening and disciplining procedures during filibusters, and particularly the prefilibuster tactics recently in evidence, must be new priorities. The time for rules of germaneness surely has arrived.

The party caucuses have already been brought into play on these procedural problems. I would think they would be a natural forum for airing the dimensions of the staggered term options that now face the upper body.

But in the final analysis it is the individual senators who have to resolve this one, and it will not be easy. James Madison wrote in the *Federalist Papers* about his concept of the members of the new Senate "whose enlightened views and virtuous sentiments render them superior to local prejudice."

The dilemma for modern-day senators is that they have leaned more and more toward the whims of public opinion, especially in matters of national and international importance. Too many legislators seem too eager, indeed, to find issues which are popular at home, rather than those which may be critical for the larger interest of the entire country.

It was Edmund Burke who warned, "Your representative owes you, not his industry alone, but his judgement, and he betrays, instead of serving you, if he sacrifices it to your opinion."

Every member of the present United States Senate ought to rally around the urgency of raising the public level of understanding in regard to the special role of a senator as a representative of the nation. The differences between the responsibilities to the citizen of a member of the House in contrast to those of a member of the Senate have to be articulated again and again. It requires the senator himself to lead his constituents to higher levels of understanding of the complexities of foreign policy problems which best serve the nation first. Former Senator J. William Fulbright has written a thoughtful monograph on this subject, "The Legislator as Educator" (*Foreign Affairs*, Volume 57, Number 4, Spring, 1979). To be sure, the senators cannot do it alone, but it remains important that they not permit their individual efforts to concentrate in opposite directions.

The senators need all the help they can get. That is why two large segments of our society outside of government have to close ranks behind the efforts of senators to assume a strong leadership role in world affairs. They are the universities and schools of the land and the national organizations and public opinion-oriented groups outside of government and academe.

The college and university programs in government, politics, and history have multiplied, particularly in enrollments. Some critics continue to suggest, however, that numerous campuses have forfeited excellence in their appeal for large enrollments. Many fine programs remain, however. American University, Georgetown University, George Washington University, and the Universities of Maryland and Virginia all contribute a wealth of materials as well as an abundance of academic and personal excellence. Multiply the potential of this central location surrounding the nation's capital by almost as many states as are across the country and one senses the larger dimension of the academic capabilities. The resulting total national dimension represents a potential reservoir of supply of present and future senators.

Particularly since the election of the new Senate class of 1958, the largest freshman class of senators in many decades, increasing numbers of members of the Senate have been identified with academic

roots—Ph.D.s, Rhodes Scholars, and the like. It would be my observation that the present 100 senators across the board are even better
prepared than the class of 1958.

But one blind side remains. There seems an increasing tendency
among the new class of senators to surrender to popular demands—to
be followers rather than leaders in foreign policy. Increased academic
emphasis on the national interest priorities of the United States Senate
would increase the odds of having higher level Senate candidacies in
both parties. Until our educational system coordinates the job description of senators with the staggered terms concept coupled with the
national interest priorities, the quality won't move upward fast
enough.

Voter education is inseparable from candidate education. Until the
public is educated to the priorities of the senator's service at the
national rather than local level, the staggered-term formula will fall
short of its purposes. National organizations, such as the League of
Women Voters, the two political parties, the Great Decision Programs, and many others, need to focus their programs more on the
integrity and capability of the candidates for United States Senator,
and to insist that they address the national interests before the local or
pedestrian questions. Agreeing with the senator ought to be secondary
to respecting him. Only under these circumstances can the better-pre-
pared members of the U.S. Senate survive the onslaught of the single-
issue groups.

And finally, there is the urgent need to inject the staggered term's
purpose into the most elementary of education levels. Most young students know, I suppose, about the bilateral legislative system of the
national Congress. But few, if any, would be aware of the special role
of a United States Senator as representative of the national interest
above and beyond local demands, at least during four of the six years.
To achieve an awareness of this principle, elementary and secondary
school teachers have to be prepared as instructors and counselors. In
addition, elementary and secondary textbooks should be reexamined
for their adequacies in focusing on this question.

A part of the problem, here, it seems to me, is not the failure in
textbooks or in classrooms to mention the formal institutional purposes of the House and Senate, but rather the failure to devote sub-
stantially *more time* and study to it in order to play catch-up with the

time that has been lost to the quickie news and the TV clichés and the current public image of the system.

Thus, in the longer run of the next fifty years, the general education level of the people's understanding of their free society and its role in the world has to be raised. The lagtime between public grasp and support of the responsibilities of world power has to be closed.

In the shorter run, the Congress and the president must—without further delay—put their respective houses in order. In the Congress it will require restoring the attributes of leaderability and at the same time positioning itself to lead public opinion in general and to motivate its constituencies in particular to respect the responsibilities of leadership. For the president, it requires genuine consultation with the Congress—no efforts at deception—and tightening up in his own house the responsibilities for policy procedures and announcements.

For the public at large, it requires the fullest understanding and support for the bilevel concept of the demands of national and international policy objectives. The requirements of a representative democracy at home must be separated from the demands of world leadership abroad. The achievability of this seeming dilemma rests as much on the state of mind as it does on the state of the Constitution.

SIX

International Youth Exchange: Completing the Public Policy Agenda

Charles MacCormack

Dr. Charles MacCormack is the president of the Experiment in International Living organization located in Brattleboro, Vermont. Dr. MacCormack has been the vice-president for programs at Save the Children Foundation and a research fellow in international relations at the Brookings Institution. In 1967–1968, Dr. MacCormack was assistant dean of international programs at Columbia University. He has served on the boards of directors of many organizations, including Partners in International Training and Education, Global Perspectives in Education, The Council on International Education Exchange, and the Global Education Fund. He has been chair of the executive committee of the Development Assistance Commission of the American Council of Volunteer Agencies for International Service. Dr. MacCormack received a Ph.D. in political science from Columbia University, and he was a Fulbright Fellow at the Universidad Central de Venezuela-Caracas. He is a member of the Council on Foreign Relations.

INTRODUCTION

For the broadest purposes of this analysis, international youth exchange will be considered to encompass all international education travel experiences to and from the United States on the part of young

106

people between the ages of sixteen and twenty-two. This includes both high school and college age exchanges, and it includes programs organized by individuals and their families, by local groups and organizations, by colleges and universities, and by national and international voluntary organizations. Although this is already a broad definition, it does not include statistics for non-U.S.- based youth exchanges—say between France and Algeria or Jamaica and the United Kingdom or the Soviet Union and Panama. To interpret fully the policy issues arising from contemporary youth exchange, it would be necessary to ascertain trends on a worldwide basis. However, since the United States continues to be the single largest actor in the youth exchange arena—although diminishing in relative importance—we will limit the present analysis to this portion of the larger issue.

WHY INTERNATIONAL YOUTH EXCHANGE?

The diminishing competencies of American young people in languages and international studies have been extensively documented and publicized over the past several years, this at a time when crucial issues of war and peace, population and ecological balance, and employment and job generation have become more and more international in their causes and solutions. And yet, according to the Chicago Council on Foreign Relations, in the 1950s 70 percent of our population felt the United States should pursue an activist policy in the world, while by 1982 this number had diminished to 54 percent. Given the accelerating development of a global marketplace, this decreasing interest and competence in languages and international involvement does not bode well for the nation's economic leadership a generation or two into the future. Fortunately, the current public concern about the general decline in academic performance in our schools, particularly in comparison with our principal economic rivals, is sparking some renewal of interest in improving our dismal record in languages and international studies.

As will be pointed out later in this paper, the individuals involved in organized youth exchange programs number in the hundreds of thousands. Over a million Americans are involved annually as members of host families. Long-term exchange students are studying in tens of thousands of American high schools every year. Additional thousands of teachers have an opportunity for personal involvement with other languages and cultures as a result of serving as group leaders for youth and student exchange programs.

Research has demonstrated the kind of positive impact exchange programs have on language competence, interest in and information about world issues, and, in many cases, long-term civic and professional involvement in international affairs. In fact, it is likely that youth and student exchange serves as the seedbed for our entire national exchange and international affairs competencies: that future teachers of languages, area studies specialists, Fulbright Professors, and other international affairs leaders in government, business and the non-profit sector have had their preliminary interest in the outside world translated into a career commitment as a result of their youth exchange experiences. Additionally, given what we know about how much young people learn from interaction with their peers, it is likely that incoming exchange students in U.S. schools, as well as returning outbound exchange students, have an important role in preserving what is left of an interest in international studies among American young people.

In sum, youth exchange is a phenomenon involving millions of people and hundreds of millions of dollars every year. It probably involves more Americans, and a broader socioeconomic spectrum of Americans, than any other form of people-to-people diplomacy. For a variety of reasons, however, youth and student exchange has failed to have the kind of impact on school systems, youth attitudes, and priority foreign policy issues most concerned people would like to see. Nevertheless, the possibilities for greatly expanding desirable public policy outcomes for relatively small incremental investments, through leveraging the already-large sums privately allocated to youth exchange are among our great untapped national resources in terms of public diplomacy. Building a consensus that youth exchange does, in fact, constitute a legitimate and unique resource for public diplomacy, identifying the most important of the desired outcomes, and agreeing on a strategy for their achievement constitutes the crucial next step on the public agenda for youth exchange.

VARIETIES OF INTERNATIONAL YOUTH EXCHANGE

The task of examining U.S.-based incoming and outbound exchanges is a formidable one. To begin with, there is no generally accepted analytical framework and no reliable data base available through which to formulate youth exchange policy. To outline some of the major variables involved in a typology of international youth exchange, there are (1) nature of program sponsorship (individually or family sponsored, locally sponsored, organizationally sponsored/travel oriented, organizationally sponsored/educationally oriented, government sponsored), (2) high school or college age, (3) academically or nonacademically oriented, (4) long term or short term, (5) individual experience or institutional impact focused, and (6) family and community immersion versus educational travel.

To give some idea of what these criteria might mean in terms of problem definition, there are over two million United States passports outstanding for the sixteen- to twenty-two-year-old age group. It is reasonable to assume that the majority of these people have invested in a passport because they will, in fact, travel to another country sometime during their formative years. The large majority of these individuals are traveling on their own, without program structure or outside financial assistance. Most of them are going to Canada, Mexico, or Western Europe.

In many cases, they are presumably expanding their knowledge of other cultures and languages, although no one really knows to what extent unprogrammed youth travel serves to reinforce existing stereotypes and prejudices as compared to broadening and deepening knowledge, insight, and skills. What is clear, however, is that a broad definition of educational youth travel immediately reveals that there is already a multimillion-dollar marketplace at work.

BASIC FACTS ABOUT YOUTH EXCHANGE

When we turn to organizationally sponsored youth exchanges, we find that there are those sponsored by local civic, school, or church groups; those sponsored by colleges and universities; and those sponsored by national organizations, some exclusively exchange oriented, some carrying out youth exchange as one part of a more specialized program thrust (such as Rotary or the Boy Scouts). Little is known about the size and nature of locally sponsored exchanges.

In terms of those sponsored by colleges, universities, and youth exchange organizations, however, we know that at least 100,000 high school age young people participate in organized outbound educational exchange programs and that they are joined by a roughly equal number of college and university students on study abroad programs. The number of incoming exchange students in this age group is even more uncertain, although a reasonable estimate might be 100,000 in the high school age group, joined by at least 200,000 in the undergraduate age group. There are, therefore, at least half a million young people between the ages of sixteen and twenty-two currently involved each year in organizationally sponsored exchanges to and from the United States.

Along with rough estimates of the numbers involved, there are several other things we know about youth exchange. One is that when it is well planned, well organized, and well implemented, it has a major impact on the values, interest in world affairs, language competence, and career choices of those involved. In the words of President Reagan, the youth exchange experience "can light the rest of our lives, elevating our ideas, deepening our tolerance, and sharpening our appetite for knowledge about the rest of the world." We also know that relatively few American young people visit Asia, Latin America, Africa, and the Middle East, where three-quarters of the world's population is located, where the most rapidly growing segment of our export market is based, and where the majority of the international conflicts of the past twenty years have been located. We know that most high school age exchanges are short term, most college and university exchanges longer term. Most youth exchanges, because they are privately funded, involve the relatively well-to-do sectors of the various nations involved.

BACKGROUND AND TRENDS IN YOUTH EXCHANGE

Fifty-two years ago when my own organization, The Experiment in International Living, "invented" the homestay and the concept of organized youth exchange, only a small handful of individuals had the opportunity to experience other languages and cultures firsthand. That generation of young people ended up experiencing the battlefields of Europe, North Africa, Asia, and the Pacific as their variation on international youth exchange. It was, in fact, that generation of World War II veterans who built the foundations of youth exchange as we know it today. Having experienced what happens when nations fail to find a way to reconcile their differences through peaceful channels, returning veterans from World War II were instrumental in building AFS, The Experiment in International Living, Youth for Understanding, and Rotary from a base of under 1,000 exchange students prior to World War II, to over 20,000 by the mid-1950s.

During these postwar years of reconstruction in Europe and anticolonial agitation in much of the rest of the world, it is likely that a significant number of all youth exchange was conducted under the auspices of a half-dozen leading international organizations, all U.S.-led. It is worth emphasizing, in fact, that modern youth exchange has historically been led by American voluntary organizations and that its emphasis on private sponsorship, volunteer support, individual self-reliance, and belief in citizen responsibility and impact has represented a unique contribution to American public diplomacy. United States private sector organizations continue to play the leading role in organized youth exchange worldwide; however, in a number of other countries such as Germany, France, Canada, the Soviet Union, and Sweden, governments are much more extensively involved than has been the case here.

In any case, by the 1960s the broad field of youth exchange began to demonstrate new characteristics: a growing volume of free-lance college student travel, a large number of study abroad programs sponsored by indivudual colleges and universities, an expansion of the number of national and special-purpose youth exchange organizations, and the entry into the field of a number of very aggressive for-profit organizations, usually relying on cash payments to teachers as the principal means of student recruitment and placement.

Finally, over the past several years, the youth exchange field appears to have entered a third phase. The principal new characteristic of this period is the expansion of family and locally organized youth exchange programs, almost certainly resulting from the growth of substantive exchange opportunities beginning in the early 1960s.

Returned Experimenters, AFSers, Peace Corps Volunteers, and Fulbrighters, having personally experienced the life-changing impact of youth exchange and having developed the personal connections and competencies to organize small exchange programs through their own earlier experiences, have created a second generation "echo" through locally sponsored initiatives.

Additionally, the present youth exchange era is characterized by the entrenchment of for-profit organizations and their nonprofit subsidiaries as major actors in the youth exchange sector, the entry of both publicly and privately administered non-U.S.-based organizations onto the American scene, the continued importance of individual student summer travel to Western Europe, the entry of the American government into the youth exchange sector in a serious way through the President's International Youth Exchange Initiative, the Congress-Bundestag Project, a host of congressional proposals for projects such as U.S.-Soviet, U.S.-Chinese, and language-focused undergraduate youth exchanges, and efforts to bring more coherence to the field through the formation of professional associations such as the Consortium for International Citizen Exchange and the International Educational Exchange Liaison Group.

Today's youth exchange field is, therefore, marked by a number of key variables:

1. Young people and their families from the United States and around the world are prepared to spend hundreds of millions of dollars of their personal funds on international educational programs to and from the United States.
2. A growing portion of this youth exchange is organized at the local level, often by individuals who themselves participated in earlier exchange programs.
3. Only a small portion of these programs are designed to have systematic impact on structures such as schools, civic associations, and the media.
4. The programs are uneven in quality: some may actually produce negative reactions; some spark an interest in languages, cross-cultural issues, and world affairs, but include little substantive content; and some, particularly at the college and university level and among the national high school exchange organizations, do provide in-depth language and area studies content.

5. This fundamentally market-driven phenomenon produces some highly skewed enrollment patterns: U.S. outbound students going primarily to Western Europe, Canada, Mexico, and Israel, very few to Eastern Europe and the Soviet Union, Asia and the Pacific, or the Third World; incoming students arrive principally from Western Europe, Japan, and the elite of the newly industrializing nations, such as Korea, Malaysia, Venezuela, Mexico, Brazil, and Saudi Arabia.

6. The structure of the field is characterized by perhaps a dozen large national organizations (both nonprofit and for-profit) programming thousands of students each, scores of small national organizations and college programs, and an even larger number of decentralized regional and local initiatives.

7. Beyond the broadest of trends and orders of magnitude, there is no central data base that provides reliable quantitative and qualitative information on the youth exchange field.

PUBLIC POLICY IMPLICATIONS OF TODAY'S YOUTH EXCHANGE FIELD

In the international exchange field, where the costs of Fulbright, Humphrey, and International Visitor exchanges often amount to tens of thousands of dollars per participant, the leveraging possibilities inherent in the already enormous private funding base for youth exchange are significant. Given this potential attractiveness of international youth exchange as a cost-effective tool of international public diplomacy and domestic educational improvement, why has it been ignored for so long as a part of our national exchange policy? There are certainly no established answers to this question, but some of the following explanations might constitute a start.

1. It simply is not considered important enough in the scheme of our national priorities for public sector funding to merit the allocation of scarce resources.

2. Private funding is already adequately supporting an important public purpose.

3. An appropriate and useful division of labor between private and public funding has not been adequately defined.

4. The benefits are primarily limited to individuals, and public funding for international education should be focused on programs that have institutional impact.

5. The field is too complex, decentralized, diverse, difficult to reach, and divided to be amenable to useful public policy interventions.
6. The goals are diffuse, the concrete outcomes difficult to measure, and adequate supporting research and data impossible to come by.
7. The possible rationales and potential beneficiaries for public support of youth exchange are so extensive and varied that it is impossible to know where to begin. It represents an insurmountable opportunity.
8. It is a "no win" situation bureaucratically and politically. The field is so extensive yet fragmented that a program that assists any particular subgroup will only leave a far larger group frustrated.
9. There is presently no organized or politically effective constituency or lobby for youth exchange. Therefore, regardless of the merits or possibilities, youth exchange loses out in the crucible of practical politics. A large number of people believe in and support youth exchange, but it is a pressing priority for very few.

Although this represents a mixed bag of arguments and explanations, there can be little doubt that in one combination or another they have long blocked any significant public sector involvement in the youth exchange field. Perhaps the factor that is most in need of improvement before a long-term strategy for youth exchange can be identified is policy-oriented research and data base development. Some of the needed information is strictly quantitative. What is the precise number of fifteen- to twenty-two-year-olds traveling to and from the United States? How many of these consider themselves to be traveling to achieve educational goals? How many are going on organized exchanges? Of the organized exchanges, how many are locally sponsored? How many are sponsored by national organizations? What are the relative numbers, by high school and college age, going to different regions of the world?

My own guess is that the quantitative analysis alone would suggest some very interesting directions for public policy on youth exchanges. Among my own working hypotheses are that: (1) the total volume of youth exchanges to and from the United States is in the hundreds of thousands each year; (2) the majority are short term and lack systematic strategies for accelerated language learning or useable knowledge about international affairs; (3) very few incorporate any strategy for using exchange students to achieve an impact on institutions; and (4) the vast majority of youth exchanges are to and from a very limited number of countries, leaving the rest of the world relatively untouched.

These hypotheses need to be tested against hard data. If they are true, however, they certainly suggest some productive public sector investment strategies: the production and dissemination of self-instructional language and cross-cultural learning materials, incentives for adding language and area studies components to existing exchange programs, incentives to expand exchanges to important but little-visited parts of the world, and publicity and merit awards for programs that have had exceptional success in using exchange students to impact significantly on community or educational institutions.

There is also a pressing need for more qualitative data on youth exchange. The most important analysis would examine a range of desired outcomes (improved language competence, increased knowledge of other cultures, expanded appreciation of cultural differences, increased interest in world affairs) against the main types of exchange experiences (individually implemented, short term travel oriented, short term educationally oriented, long term educationally oriented). We also need longitudinal data that examine factors such as choice of academic major and career, involvement in the international dimensions of one's profession, ongoing participation in or support for international programs, and level of success in any subsequent international endeavors against having been or not been an exchange student and against different types of exchange programs. These data would provide significant guidance as to the most cost-effective form of public investment in youth exchange.

I believe that a useable base of policy-oriented research and data could be gathered without a tremendous expenditure of time, energy, or money. A reliable outline of the major quantitative and qualitative patterns could probably be pieced together from existing data, already completed research projects, and a carefully selected and limited body of new research commissioned to fill in gaps in essential information.

It would not have to be a highly sophisticated research effort, but it would provide the information needed to make intelligent choices among the alternative uses of limited public funds for youth exchange. Such a policy-oriented research overview would have to be coordinated by the U.S. Information Agency, which would finalize the overall design, compile existing data and research, and commission the remaining work to be done.

The important thing is that the data be available to assist us in making informed choices. The tremendous private investment in international youth exchange is too valuable a potential asset not be capitalized on as an important tool of public diplomacy. The specific priorities for youth exchange programs at any given time (for example, impact on the quality of public school language and social studies teaching, improving future relations with our key economic allies, building a better base of future professional leaders capable of functioning in important but little-known·languages, or reducing the risk of unintended superpower confrontation throught expanded East/West interaction among young people) can be sorted out through the ongoing dynamics of the political process. The need at the present time is to institutionalize the current tentative recognition of international youth exchange as an important and legitimate component of our national exchange policy and our foreign policy.

THE PRESIDENT'S INTERNATIONAL
YOUTH EXCHANGE INITIATIVE

Until 1982 the evolution of youth exchange to and from the United States was exclusively determined by the dynamics of the private and voluntary sectors. In that year, President Reagan and USIA Director Charles Wick, preparing for the 1982 Economic Summit Conference at Versailles, noted that there were significant differences between different age groups in the level of support for cooperation among the major industrialized democracies with young people far less likely to be supportive of joint action than their elders.

This finding was consistent with what had already been defined by foreign policy scholars as the ''successor generation'' issue—the fact that the patterns of cooperation and communication that had been forged among young leaders of the World War II period were not being replicated among today's young people.

The presidents and prime ministers of Canada, the United States, France, Germany, Italy, Great Britain, and Japan, gathered at Versailles, unanimously endorsed the American proposal that the

1982–1985 period should see a doubling of educationally oriented youth exchanges between the United States and the other six economic summit countries.

Many of these governments had already recognized the value of supplementing the private and voluntary sectors' roles in youth exchange, where market forces were not adequately achieving the full range of public policy goals. For example, since World War II, France and Germany have sponsored what is probably the world's biggest organized youth exchange program as one means of countering the century of bloody and bitter enmity that characterized relations between their two countries through 1945. Canada has long sponsored youth and student exchanges to and from the Third World. Japan has funded Youth for Understanding to expand the number of promising American young people having in-depth experiences in Japan. Although our major economic partners naturally have different priorities as to what specific form their sponsorship of expanded youth exchanges might take, all clearly welcomed a positive and creative American initiative in this sector.

The implementation strategy of the President's International Youth Exchange Initiative was also well designed to capture the unique leveraging possibilities of this field. First, it utilized the existing capacities of the already established organizations in the field. Their hundreds of thousands of experienced volunteers and alumni in this and the other economic summit countries represented a virtually irreplaceable asset. The high-level recognition of a cause for which so many had long worked constituted an important source of motivation for youth exchange volunteers.

Second, rather than providing direct scholarships or subsidies, the initiative has focused on programs that would build enrollments and program quality on a self-sustaining, long-term basis. During a period when inflation, the strong dollar, high college tuition, diminishing numbers of volunteers, and career anxiety among young people have all combined to reduce the rate of growth of youth exchanges to and from the United States, the goal of long-term enrollment expansion is a timely intervention. The concept of venture capital to enable the field to achieve public policy goals constitutes an imaginative and cost-effective strategy for the youth exchange sector.

Third, the initiative has supported activities that could only be done in behalf of the field as a whole, that no single organization or group of organizations could do separately. For example, the initiative has created a high-level President's Council of corporate and civic leaders and implemented a national fund-raising campaign under the leadership of Coy Eklund of Equitable Life. This campaign has certainly increased the visibility of international exchange among corporate and foundation donors, a visibility that, hopefully, will result in a permanent increase in funding to a field that has had difficulty in attracting the attention of the large donor community over the past twenty years. The component of the initiative that could potentially have the greatest long-term benefit of all is the national mass media advertising campaign which is using television, radio, and print to increase broad public awareness of the advantages of either being or hosting an exchange student. The market value of this campaign has been estimated to be in the range of $50 to $75 million, but through the *pro bono* services of the Advertising Council and the advertising agency of Richardson, Meyers and Donofrio, the cost in out-of-pocket government revenues has been very small.

There is little doubt that the President's International Youth Exchange Initiative will succeed in achieving its goal of doubling organized youth exchanges between the United States and our economic summit partners within three years. Even within this limited time frame, the per capita costs to the government of these additional exchanges will be under $750, and the final figure will probably be significantly less. Realizing also that the expanded number of youth exchanges will represent a new plateau that should be able to be sustained long into the future without the need for permanent subsidies, the ultimate per capita cost of each new exchange generated by the initiative falls even further.

Additionally, if the advertising campaign succeeds in broadening and deepening general public interest in youth exchange, not only will participation with the economic summit countries be doubled, but exchanges with other parts of the world should also increase as a desirable by-product. Since high school exchange students are likely to become college exchange students, and since exchange students in general are likely to be interested in and support international education, the entire field benefits.

THE IMPACT OF THE INTERNATIONAL
YOUTH EXCHANGE INITIATIVE

The single greatest impact of the International Youth Exchange Initiative has probably been to put youth and student exchange on the agenda of government policymakers in this country and around the world. Because of the high-level American interest, other goverments have, often for the first time, taken a serious look at youth exchange. Even those governments that have been actively involved in the past appear to have been surprised by the scale, diversity, and complexity of what they have discovered. There also appears to have been increased recognition of the broad-based constituency for youth exchange—that citizens who might never have an opportunity to be involved in or benefit from scholarly or technical exchanges can still play an important role in youth exchange. Congress has also recognized the potential of youth exchange programs: they have funded the Congress/Bundestag Youth Exchange Program, and bills are pending for a number of other new youth exchange programs.

The Youth Exchange Initiative will, therefore, succeed in reaching its goal of doubling exchanges among the economic summit countries, and it has also sparked a new and growing interest in the possibilities of youth exchange as a cost-effective tool of public diplomacy. Nevertheless, much still needs to be done before the initiative can accomplish all that it is capable of. Continued leadership is needed to promote the value of youth exchange as a serious dimension of public diplomacy, both as a uniquely cost-effective approach and as a seedbed for later leadership in international affairs. A modest breakthrough has been achieved by the initiative, but there continues to be considerable skepticism or disinterest in many quarters. To counter this, there needs to be a clearer enunciation by USIA of its long-term goals and priorities for youth exchange, not only regarding the economic summit countries but also in other key areas such as the acquisition of critical languages or the expansion of knowledge and understanding in the North-South and East-West spheres. It will also be necessary to complete the process of gathering the data to verify the impacts of youth exchange.

Beyond this, the outlines of a long-term exchange policy should include the following objectives:

1. Institutionalize the impact of the economic summit countries–oriented phase so as to sustain enrollment levels for the long run.
2. Continue the national advertising campaign until it achieves a major impact on the potential exchange student and host family audience.
3. Expand into high-priority, low-market-interest countries, particularly North-South and also East-West.
4. Where necessary, diversify the initiative rationale (such as for Third World exchanges, where service or vocational approaches would be more appropriate).
5. Sustain the venture capital strategy wherever possible in order to avoid long-term dependency on government funding.
6. Clearly incorporate well-focused undergraduate college and university programs into the initiative.

All of this will serve to establish youth exchange as an additional dimension of our national exchange policy, one that is unique in terms of leveraging private funds and providing a base for future leadership in international affairs.

Several decades ago, H. G. Wells noted that "History is a race between education and survival." We would do young people a disservice if we failed to provide them with the tools and experiences they need not only to survive but to flourish in the global village they are inheriting.

Setting the course for doing this and seeing it through will constitute completing the public policy agenda for international youth exchange.

SEVEN

Educating Tomorrow's Leaders
For An Uncertain World

Richard M. Krasno

Dr. Richard M. Krasno is the president and chief executive officer of the Institute of International Education located at the United Nations Plaza in New York City. He was the deputy assistant secretary of education for international education with the U.S. Department of Education and was with the Ford Foundation in the Office of the Vice-President, where he coordinated international education activities worldwide for the foundation. In 1973–1974, Dr. Krasno was a Fulbright Professor of Educational Psychology at the Universidad de Santiago, Santiago de Compostela, Spain. He has taught at London University, the University of Chicago, Stanford University, and the University of Massachusetts. Dr. Krasno has his Ph.D. from Stanford University.

What *is* leadership? Guiding, directing, commanding, as the dictionary defines it? What is leadership for an individual? Or for a nation?

For a nation, is it economic and military predominance? Technological preeminence? I choose to define leadership for our purposes as the capacity to understand and respond to change beyond one's borders. I would argue that this definition is the key to lasting leadership, especially in the latter part of the twentieth century. While the United States is still strong, economically and technologically our predominance has diminished. Some 70 percent of our domestic production is exposed to foreign competition. Yet most of us continue to act as if the world that counts ended at our borders.

It might be argued that it doesn't matter if most of us know nothing about what goes on beyond the city limits of Washington or Cincinnati or Fresno, as long as our national leaders—in business and education and civic life as well as in government—have a more expansive world view. Unfortunately, all too often this is not the case. Career preparation for law and business and academe typically does not offer its highest rewards to the internationalist.

Nor is "educating tomorrow's leaders for an uncertain world" a sufficient statement of the problem we face. Leadership in international affairs cannot be developed or exerted in a vacuum. Effective leadership in a democracy emerges from a context of informed public opinion and debate. In the United States, in 1984, a good case can be made that the majority of U.S. citizens—and a significant proportion of our leadership—lack the capacity to understand and respond to international issues.

I am convinced that more effective international leadership will emerge only when those of us who are led understand why and how international issues affect our daily lives. Only then will we demand a more farsighted approach to international decision making. Only then will we be building the context and capability for international leadership in America.

We are a large and complex nation, and international education is a large and complex task for this country. It encompasses global issues education in the elementary and secondary schools and foreign language training at all levels; foreign student education and U.S. youth studying abroad; area studies and international studies and comparative studies; postgraduate scholarly exchanges; education for development; training for international business and the professions; ethnic studies, bilingual education, and the teaching of English as a second language.

"Education for international leadership" is the type of omnibus theme, covering most of the issues I just listed, that is rather frequently assigned to those presumed to have expertise in it. I think that is because we are presumed to have a world view, a *worldwide* view, as senior managers of this country's largest higher educational exchange agency. One's temptation, in responding, is to provide a tour of the horizon, pointing with horror at the undoubted weaknesses of international education in America, pointing with pride at the many initiatives designed to make things better, and winding up with a resounding description of an ideal future in which goverment, foundations, corporations, education, and the community rise to the global challenge in an unparalleled display of wisdom and unity.

I would hope to avoid that, although I can't avoid touring the horizon altogether if I am to illuminate the topic. What interest me, perhaps because of my backround in educational psychology, are the *signals* and *motivators* required to build America's international capability.

First, let me explain what I mean by signals and motivators. *Signals* emerge at the national level, when a consensus on a policy issue begins to form. Now the United States can in no way be said to have, nor should it have, an international education policy. Given our decentrally pluralistic form of government, we can be said to have very few national policies. What emerges more often than a consistent national policy is a set of more or less consistent signals. We are seeing this happen right now, I believe, as diverse sectors of our society address the issue of excellence in education. Twenty-five years ago the parallel issue was the management of decline. In the mid-1980s, we have a flurry of policy studies and polemics addressing the need to improve the quality of our diminished educational enterprise.

Legislators and the media at all levels—national, state, and local— are picking up the signals. As a result, for the remainder of the 1980s we as a country are likely to see a higher priority for education than has been the case for two decades.

A signal, then, is a shift in the national mood significant enough to mobilize action and funding. In our pluralistic society, numerous conflicting interest groups must overlook their differences and send broadly similar signals before the President, Congress, and the media can begin to sell change to the larger public.

Signals are *national* in character; motivators are *individual*. I can best illustrate the difference by citing the numerous attempts to legislate morality in this country, the best of all possible examples being Prohibition. In this case, religious and temperance groups backed by a conservative citizenry raised on Puritanical principles of personal conduct persuaded legislators that abstinence was in the national interest. The idea that sobriety indubitably equals health, wealth, and productivity was a suitably Calvinist position in the Victorian afterglow of the early twentieth century.

The Prohibition Amendment immediately foundered just because it

was a *prohibition*—a prescriptive approach to morality that paid no
attention to individual motivations. Ironically, but predictably, Prohibition had the opposite effect, offering a rebel's motivation to drink
even to those who had never indulged heavily before. "Up the individual!"—even at the price of one's liver. That continues to be the
American way.

My point: national signals must coincide with the pragmatic motivations of individuals and interest groups before large-scale change
can take place in our society. Stated simply, this seems axiomatic, but
it's an axiom frequently overlooked by the high-minded in a society
heavily given to prescriptive solutions.

Returning from the evils of drink to the more exciting topic of
international education, where are we now, in a snapshot dated April
1984? Prescriptively, international education is good. There are some
very encouraging signals that indicate that the connection between
international leadership and international education is becoming
established in the minds of the Congress and other power nexus.
Descriptively, however, what motivation is there for the major sectors
of society to invest real dollars in international education in the economically and politically uncertain environment of the 1980s?

I can bring you some good news and some bad news. The good
news first.

THE FEDERAL GOVERNMENT AND NATIONAL SECURITY: SIGNALS AND MOTIVATORS COINCIDE

Just at this moment, the federal government's commitment to the
value of international educational *exchange* to our foreign policy and
our national security is probably at its highest point in twenty years.
In recent times the Congress has pushed for a twofold increase of the
Fulbright Program and an expansion of the International Visitor Program, which brings distinguished foreign nationals to the United
States. The President has established his Youth Initiative, which
hopes to use the exchange mechanism to build better relations with
the "successor generation" of young leaders in the allied nations of
Western Europe, Japan, and some less developed nations. The
Kissinger Commission has proposed, and Congress shows an inclina-

tion to fund, a remarkably larger exchange effort in Central American countries.

The present Administration is sending a clear signal that exchange is a positive means of building friends for our society. It has abundant practical motivation for doing so: the Soviet Union, Cuba, and other Eastern block nations are educating large numbers of foreign nationals as a strategic investment. The United States can do no less, if it is to win the battle for people's minds.

What is the "best case" outlook here? I hope that the renewed commitment to exchange will finally take its proper place as a more permanent priority of our national government. Whether one agrees with all aspects of the current Administration's policies or not, it is very hard to disagree with its perception that international educational exchange has a permanent and positive effect on foreign perceptions of America.

The United States has a special opportunity to test this assumption now in relation to its traditional allies. The recent growth of our relationship with Western Europe and Japan has largely been in terms of technology, trade, and defense. The immigrant ties to these cultures are quite literally dying out. Culturally we are in a period of estrangement, especially with respect to the younger people who don't remember World War II.

I would plead for greatly expanded scholarly and, especially, *nonscholarly* exchanges with these nations. Power is diffused in industrialized nations. Expanded nonscholarly exchanges should reach opinion leaders and decision-makers in all sectors of society—the media, the lower and middle levels of government, labor, management, small entrepreneurs and farmers, secondary and elementary school teachers, and many other groups with lesser access to exchange opportunities. The President's Youth Initiative is a step in the right direction. I hope the concept will be taken further.

I would also make a special plea that the participation of the American people in such exchanges be enhanced. For the federal government, there is a natural inclination to see investment in exchange as being of greatest importance on the foreign side. However, individual American citizens make excellent ambassadors for our culture and values. Moreover, opinion leaders in America—journalists, local officials, business executives, and representatives of many other sectors of our society—would benefit enormously from organized exposure to their counterparts in Western Europe and Japan. They are often much more parochial in outlook than their counterparts overseas.

The concept of an International Visitor Program in reverse is not a new one, but remains an excellent idea. Pop culture and casual tourism are rather obviously insufficient for building the bonds of understanding and trust between the successor generations in the United States, Europe, and Japan. Building those bonds of trust is a crucially important task in assuring our national future.

Initiatives in this direction are likely to be welcomed by our friends in Europe and Japan, who are more aware than we of the dangers of inadequate communication. As Robert Christopher, former editor of *Newsweek International*, noted in a recent speech in Japan:

> *Even the best American universities have provided the vast majority of their students with little, if any exposure to Asian affairs in general and even less to Japanese history and culture in particular. . . . While the extraordinary intimacy of the economic and political ties that have grown up between Japan and the United States has impelled a certain number of Americans to remedy this deficiency through self-education . . . great numbers of otherwise well-informed Americans are still only partially aware of the true nature of the Japanese-American relationship and of its important to America's own well-being . . . . I very much doubt that one American in five hundred is aware that Japan is the biggest importer of U.S. agricultural products, including U.S. beef. Neither workers nor management in the U.S. steel industry pays very much attention to the evidence that it is not so much foreign competition but U.S. industry's own failure to invest and modernize that lies at the root of its troubles. One of the many unfortunate results of this widespread ignorance of Japan is that those Americans who seek to lay primary blame for our country's economic difficulties at Japan's feet have relatively clear sailing. The forcefulness and seeming authority with which they speak almost inevitably impresses other Americans, including politicans, bureaucrats, and editorial writers, who have no independent basis on which to judge the assertions of protectionists.*

Exchange can provide that independent basis on which to judge. German Ambassador Peter Hermes made the point most eloquently in a recent speech when he observed that:

What we on both sides of the Atlantic ultimately share is not only a common interest in defense or even the strong economic ties which bind us together. Our main tie is the message of hope and progress provided by the democratic ideal. I am quite certain that young people on both sides of the Atlantic share many of the same hopes and aspirations [but] we have to promote understanding between our nations, and in particular between our younger generations.

Without such sharing, we face the danger not so much of isolationism, but of a growing *unilateralism* in our society founded on parochialism and ignorance. Expanded citizen and leader exchanges could do much to alleviate the problem on both sides.

THE FEDERAL GOVERNMENT AND THE LESS-DEVELOPED COUNTRIES: MIXED SIGNALS AND MIXED MOTIVATIONS

Where our national security is concerned, our government's signals and motivations are clear. The signal is pro-exchange. The motivation is clearly strategic: to build friendly ties with both our traditional allies and the more strategically sensitive developing nations.

The national security argument is somewhat of a two-edged sword, however, as it applies to the less developed countries (LDCs) *overall*. The implication is that some LDCs are strategically sensitive while others are not. In a globally interdependent world, this seems—to me at least—to be an unfortunate distinction. It also encourages an essentially reactive American policy in regard to educating the future leaders of the developing nations.

Make no mistake about it: educating LDC nationals *is* education for leadership. The governing groups of these countries are disproportionately drawn from the few who have been trained abroad. It may be argued that the United States is training a great many more LDC nationals than the Soviets are (270,000 as opposed to approximately 90,000); however, virtually all 90,000 Soviet-assisted foreign students receive Soviet government grants. Well under 10,000 LDC students in the United States receive such support.

LDC students in the United States come disproportionately from a rather small group of the more economically advantaged developing

nations. Because most pay their own way, they are also disproportionately drawn from economically privileged groups. The Soviets
can, and do, seek to reach a broader range of potential leaders from
less advantaged sectors of society through their international training
program.

In this regard, it is worth observing that greater exchange funding
could have built friends for the United States in Central America several administrations ago, had we not pursued such a purely reactive
policy. This is not to fault the present Administration, which deserves
praise for finally acting on this realization after several previous
administrations did not.

It is an unfortunate truism that foriegn assistance lacks a constituency in this country. What this means, in effect, is that only countries
now teetering on the brink of communism receive much United States
investment in international training. That hardly strikes foreign governments as a sustained commitment to education for development.
Executive branch recommendations have hardly ever been followed
by increased congressional funding in the past fifteen years, a decidedly mixed signal to send to the LDCs.

The U.S. Agency for International Development and the U.S.
Information Agency, through such mechanisms as the USAID Participant Training Program and the USIA Humphrey Fellowships, do
yeoman service in extending what resources are made available.
USAID has been ingenious in stretching funds through shorter
grants, more in-country training, more practical training, and other
means. To really do their job fully, however, the executive branch
agencies need sustained congressional support that has not been
forthcoming.

SUNY Chancellor Clifton Wharton put the problem eloquently in
his keynote address to the most recent meeting of the American Association of State Colleges and Universities:

> *Federal support for overseas assistance has declined sharply . . . yet the
> problem of development is one of the world's great challenges in this coun-
> try—perhaps the great challenge, in that development seeks to address the
> hunger, poverty, and ignorance that lie at the roots of so much global tension
> and discord . . . . In reducing our commitment to development, we
> reduce our own role in and contribution to a world-scale change that has no*

precedent and no analogue in the entire chronicle of human history.

Is there sufficient motivation for a change in U.S. policy? Realistically, it is hard to perceive it. Our signals are mixed because we often
confuse foreign assistance with charity, when it is more accurately
perceived as investment. This is especially the case in the training of
the next leadership generation in the LDCs.

John F. Kennedy felt that it was sufficient motivation to offer development assistance "because it is right." Unfortunately, that seems
too abstract to legislators dealing with many competing domestic
demands for very scarce tax dollars. One is left with the hope that the
developing nations will remain neutral or friendly, rather than
become actively hostile to American interests. But if they do, it is
often more a matter of luck than of effective American foreign policy.

Here again, an increased U.S. exchange presence could prove
invaluable. In the "best case" scenario, enhanced scholarly and
nonscholarly exchanges focused on the LDCs would assist in building
the case for development assistance among the American people in
general. People-to-people contacts make real such abstract notions as
hunger in the Sahel or environmental degradation in Nepal. I am
reminded of the role returned Peace Corps volunteers have played in
organizing and sustaining whatever limited grassroots support for
development assistance still exists in the United States.

I would also like to bring to your attention a new IIE (Institute of
International Education) study, published in April 1984, entitled
Fondness and Frustration. *Fondness and Frustration* is the product of a series
of interviews conducted by Duke University Graduate Dean Craw-
furd Goodwin and Harvard University Professor Michael Nacht with
Brazilian alumni of U.S. higher education.

The study demonstrates in no uncertain terms the positive value of
U.S. education to indivdual Brazilians and to Brazil as a nation. The
Brazilian alumni felt the experience was crucial to their career preparation and personal development. Their increased understanding of
our society and political system has affected their thinking about
America throughout life. The experience encouraged sustained economic and academic ties with the U.S., and many said that their
exposure to the problem-solving approach of United States science
and the open debate in United States classrooms had totally changed

their mode of thought. It is hard to imagine a more eloquent testimony to the value of U.S. education to a developing nation than this book. Let us now turn our attention to American educational institutions and their role in international education.

AMERICAN EDUCATION AND INTERNATIONAL EDUCATION: FINDING A NEW RATIONALE

As far as educational *exchange* is concerned, I perceive the federal government's signals in regard to our traditional allies and strategic developing nations as positive, and the signals in regard to the developing world overall as somewhat mixed. But what of the federal government in its role in relation to the international education of Americans—in American schools and universities?

There are some promising signals here also. Congressman Paul Simon has been particularly tireless in support of foreign language and international studies. His Foreign Language Assistance for National Security legislation, introduced in 1983, would institute a program of capitation grants to higher education based on foreign language enrollments and requirements. The legislation seeks to promote model language programs at elementary and secondary schools, and community colleges, set up institutes to improve skills of language teachers, and increase the linkages between language learning and career fields such as business and engineering. Congressman Simon has also sought to build an international education component into the reauthorized Higher Education Act, for which he began conducting hearings last fall.

Already underway through the U.S. Department of Education is an innovative program to encourage international business education. The U.S. Information Agency has recently begun a project to build university-to-university linkages with overseas institutions, and other useful experiments are underway.

National policy leaders and advocacy groups have also not been idle. President Michael Sovern of Columbia University recently proposed a National Endowment for International Studies. There have been proposals to use reflow funds for exchanges and for international studies. Global Perspectives in Education, a major agency in developing the global education resources of American schools, convened a national conference in May 1984, that brought together representatives of hundreds of organizations concerned with international affairs education.

The National Council for Foreign Language and International Studies has done especially notable work in its short life in placing international studies on our national agenda. It has issued a series of influential reports which have provided a strong rationale for all of us concerned with enhancing the international capacities of Americans. It has published case studies of effective programs, has sponsored interface committees that have brought together educators with business executives and other important international actors in the American community, and deserves much credit for the revitalization of interest in foreign language and international studies in the media and in the community.

Activity should not be confined to the national level. Many states have recently revitalized their commitment to international education. As Rose Hayden, head of the National Council on Foreign Language and International Studies, reports in a recent article about such efforts:

> *Reports tend to . . . focus on the economic rade and cultural dimensions of the particular state, and recommend actions to state and local authorities and educators. By and large, the reports have set lofty, far-reaching goals rather than specific objectives that can be put into operation. But to the extent that statewide initiatives and surveys have business and political representation, these new reports have good odds of being visible to broader publics, and of being implemented.*

Dr. Hayden's quotation is suggestive in a number of ways. First of all, its point about the states really applies to the new international education movement as a whole. We are just now in the report stage. There are many experiments underway, and innovative work is being done. It is a struggle, however, that has just begun.

The task facing those of us committed to international education in the schools and colleges is daunting. Federal funding, the good efforts of Congressman Simon aside, has been slight for many years, as has funding from the foundation community. Title VI funding has also been very fragile at best. States, too, are facing severe budget constraints, and have found it difficult to follow up the reports of international education study groups with much funding. Local communities face parallel problems in affording appropriate programs.

The new emphasis on excellence in education is likely to have a positive effect on the state and local scene, especially on elementary and secondary education, as greater emphasis is placed on educating Americans for their place in the world. Colleges and universities are slowly reinstating the foreign language requirements they dropped in the 1960s and 1970s. This should prove effective in encouraging language training in the schools, as high schools will seek to maximize the admissions opportunities for which their students qualify by reinstating their own foreign language requirements.

Some of the innovative experiments underway can be expected to have a multiplier effect. Among one of the most intriguing ideas is that of the "international magnet school," of which there are a number already in existence at the secondary school level. Such schools act as focal points for international education for entire community educational systems and focus scarce resources effectively.

What do I perceive as the "best case scenario"? I see the need for continued advocacy by such groups as the National Council for Foreign Language and International Studies to keep international education visible on the national agenda. The federal government and the foundations must be encouraged to take a longer range perspective on funding needs. It seems unlikely that they will or should assume the entire burden from the states and cities, but what they *can* and *should* do is to provide fairly substantial incentive programs that would act as sources of seed money for innovation.

The elementary schools have an important role to play in awakening our children to the world outside. Secondary schools need to do likewise and to provide language training opportunities as well. Better curricular materials and improved teacher training are the keys to success here.

It should be noted that very little of this is likely to happen unless state education authorities are persuaded to pay for it. Here again, effective advocacy right down to the grassroots level is the key. National commissions can provide the arguments, but local communities must provide the impetus for change.

As for higher education, its task in educating leaders for an uncertain world has many aspects: international affairs education and language training for U.S. citizens, foreign student education, graduate training, scholarly research, the maintenance of area studies and international policy centers, technical assistance to LDC educational development projects, etc.

There is much that higher education could do to use existing resources better. For example, the 336,000 foreign students on U.S. campuses are an important but underutilized resource. They can be used much more effectively as learning resources in the classroom: they can provide a needed cosmopolitan exposure for many U.S. students.

Higher education is seeking to revitalize its mission in international education in a number of ways. There are many examples of effective international education programs in many colleges and universities, which are thriving without excessive dependence on federal dollars or other outside funding. Indeed, high-level administrative support and entrepreneurial leadership seem more important to a successful program than large federal grants.

In the near future, Richard Lambert of the University of Pennsylvania will publish a study of area and language studies centers which should help to set the agenda for these issues for the remainder of the decade. International education, therefore, is by no means a moribund field on American campuses.

It is, however, a field searching for a new mission, or at least it seems so to me. American higher education had a quarter-century of growth after World War II, followed by the shock of inflation, stagnating enrollments, and sharply higher costs. Academic hiring dwindled, academic programs were cut, and weaker institutions vanished or merged. We were visited with the phenomenon of the Ph.D. as itinerant pieceworker—a course here, a course there, with no hope of health insurance or tenure.

After a period of shock and disarray, some segments of the academic community have snapped back. For some schools it has been a salutary experience, forcing a reconsideration of academic mission that might not otherwise have brought the institution into the modern world. Admissions officers have become more aggressive. Academic departments have been forced to consider what vocational use their courses might have beyond the traditional preparation for the academic life.

"The new careerism" has its dangers, of course, as excessive numbers of the best and the brightest flee to the presumed safety of increasingly overcrowded professional schools and career-oriented majors such as business and accounting. Overall, however, I believe that the realization of the limits to growth has been a needed corrective for much of American higher education.

International education has in some ways lagged behind in dealing with this new reality. We are just now beginning to find effective means of linking international studies to the world outside the classroom. The American Assembly of Collegiate Schools of Business has been encouraging business schools to internationalize their offerings. Major universities such as the University of Pennsylvania are seeking to do likewise in regard to business education. It is still the case, however, that the great majority of our business school graduates do not take as much as a single course in international business.

Nor is our track record much better in other fields. Area studies centers have had difficulty integrating their offerings with other disciplines. The career track in most academic disciplines encourages the mainstream domestic specialist over the internationalist. International experience is not considered entirely relevant in the professional and career-oriented fields (law, accounting, health, engineering and sciences, computer studies, etc.) to which students increasingly flock.

I, personally, do not find it unimportant that universities should seek to sustain such important and traditional academic responsibilities as basic area studies research or the teaching of less commonly taught languages. After all, competence in the less commonly taught languages has a way of becoming important to our national interests fairly regularly. Consider, for example, the recent relevance of Farsi or of the Indochinese languages.

I do think, however, that as far as the larger educational role of the American university is concerned, we have yet to find a clear mission for international education beyond traditional academic and cultural goals. While many of us agree it is good to speak a foreign language because it provides a perspective on another culture unavailable in any other way, this in itself is not going to persuade vast numbers of American students to study foreign language—unless they perceive its direct relevance to their personal goals.

HIGHER EDUCATION AND BUSINESS: IS THERE
REALLY A NEED FOR INTERNATIONAL COMPETENCE

Finally, let me turn my attention to higher education and business. To again quote Rose Hayden:

> *Today U.S. investment abroad is in excess of $300 billion. Our thirteen largest banks derive almost half their total earnings from overseas credits. More than 6,000 U.S. companies have some form of operation abroad, and approximately one-third of all U.S. corporate profits come from international activities. Some 20 percent of our total national industrial production is for export. Nationwide, four out of five new jobs in manufacturing are now created as a direct result of foreign trade. One out of three acres of farmland produces for export.*
>
> *On the surface, it would appear that all is well. We are, today, the world's largest and most productive economy, the world's largest market, the world's leading exporter and importer, and the world's strongest defender of free trade. But appearances are deceiving. We are staggering under a balance-of-trade deficit in the hundreds of billions of dollars . . . . In 1960, when we were the world's largest exporter of manufactured goods, we held 25 percent of the world market . . . . Today, however, our share of the world's $2 trillion export market is down to approximately 10 percent, and we have been replaced by Germany and Japan as the leaders in world manufactured exports.*
>
> *Many factors have contributed to our slippage . . . but of all the factors, one stands out unmistakably. Relatively few American businessmen understand the culture, the customs, or even the language of the foreign buyer . . . . As a result, America's competitive edge is often lost in the tough realities of international buying and selling.*

The shock of international competition could prove to be the best thing that has happened to U.S. business in twenty years, forcing the investment in new plants and research facilities and the aggressive international marketing approaches that have won trade advantages for the Japanese and Germans in recent years. Or it could prove to be an insurmountable opportunity.

A good deal will be determined by the willingness to learn of U.S.

business executives. U.S. higher education can provide help by giving them a better backround for coping with international competition, not just through better international business schools training, but also by greater emphasis on international content in such disciplines as economics and greater emphasis on foreign language learning. (In Paris, the president of the Monterey Institute of International Studies asked a Japanese executive what language he thought most important for world trade. In flawless French, the Japanese executive replied, "Sir, the most useful international language is not necessarily English, but rather it is the language of your client.")

Higher education could also make more effective use of the exchange mechanism, organizing seminars for international business executives from both the United States and foreign sides, organizing study-abroad programs focused on business-related issues, and providing opportunities for midcareer adult learners to experience such overseas innovations as "quality circles" firsthand. More could be done on the United States campuses as well for the midcareer executive with international responsibilities, through such means as short courses, seminars, guided tutorials, and special certification programs.

These ideas are not entirely new. Prototype programs do exist. There are obstacles to their expansion in the barriers to communication that often arise between academe and the corporate world. However, it is in our national interest to overcome these obstacles. As I noted earlier, the challenge of Japan could prove to be the best thing to happen to American business, if it stimulates productivity, reindustrialization, a questioning of current labor management practices, and a renewed emphasis on quality as well as profit. This assumes, however, that American education and American business read each other's signals correctly. Educators must ask themselves whether they are producing for today's market, in international education as well as in many other academic fields and disciplines. Business executives must ask themselves whether they are learning enough about the international environment in which they work to function effectively. The recent experiences of the auto and steel industries and of our largest banks argue that this many not be so.

There *are* companies that bring a genuinely international perspective both to their business and to their community relations. ITT's sponsorship of this Key Issues Series is one example. So is ITT's

International Fellowship Program, now celebrating its tenth anniversary. ITT and the Institute of International Education have cooperated in this two-way exchange program since its inception in 1972. We recently completed an evaluation of the program.

The nearly 600 alumni provided eloquent testimony. The opportunity to study abroad clearly increased access to career options, and many participants expect to become leaders in their particular fields. As one ITT alumnus wrote:

> *Today's fellows may be tomorrow's spokespersons in areas involving international relations, and the ITT experience will have played a significant factor in their career development.*

Many ITT Fellows have indeed entered international fields, including fellows who had not expected to follow this career track prior to studying abroad.

It is particularly notable that many foreign fellows shift from other fields to business and management when they come to the United States. In many foreign countries, no such specialization exists, or it exists only at the undergraduate level. Also, U.S. business programs are often designed for students whose previous major was in another field. Among foreign ITT alumni are physicians who came here to study health care administration and engineers who pursued business administration as a useful adjunct to their technical education.

The ITT evaluation study concludes that:

> *In the public and private lives of these fellows, the overseas educational experience has a profound and lasting effect.*

ITT makes an investment in international education and international affairs that extends far beyond its business interests. We can hope that it will establish a model for corporate investment in years to come.

INTERNATIONAL EDUCATION AND THE COMMUNITY: THE NEED FOR BETTER COMMUNICATION

In conclusion, I think America's effectiveness in international business, in foreign policy, in the management of domestic issues with international implications such as agricultural policy, and its effectiveness in myriad other areas is largely dependent on an internationally aware citizenry.

The general public does have the capacity to become involved in international concerns, as volunteer efforts such as the National Council for International Visitors abundantly prove. It is largely a latent capacity, however, one that needs the right signals to motivate it.

Here again, I would argue that a greater number of nonscholarly exchanges involving Americans from many sectors of our national life coud prove highly beneficial. I would also argue for many more organized exchanges of journalists. Americans get their picture of the world from thirty-second snatches of television news and the front pages of their newspapers. International affairs are treated sketchily or not at all in many news presentations. The reasons usually given are lack of interest, lack of time, and smaller overseas news bureaus. The context and capability for international leadership in America would be strengthened immeasurably if Americans were not insulated by their news media.

European children are exposed to international influences almost from birth. They see foreigners, hear their families speak other languages, learn two or three languages in elementary and secondary school, and function in an international business environment all their lives. Both the signals and the motivators in their environment dictate a fully international commitment.

This has not been the case for Americans. The media and the schools bear a great responsibility to inform Americans about the larger world in which they will be expected to function. International education must become an integral part of our daily lives if we are to function effectively as leaders in an uncertain world. If we fail to equip ourselves properly for this important responsibility, we may be signing away our future.